Your Last Day of School

56 Ways You Can Be A Great Intern *and* Turn Your Internship Into A Job

Eric Woodard

© 2011 by Eric Woodard

All rights reserved, including the right of reproduction in whole or in part in any form.

First Edition

Edited by Cynthia Mulligan

Cover, Interior Design and Typography by Cynthia Mulligan

Library of Congress Cataloging-in-Publication Data
Woodard, Eric.

     Your last day of school: 56 ways you can be a great intern and turn your internship into a job / by Eric Woodard

     p.   cm.

     LCCN: 2011918375

     ISBN-10: 1466414200

     ISBN-13: 978-1466414204

eric@woodardweb.com   www.GreatIntern.com

LC
1072
.I55
W663
2011

Montante Family Library
D'Youville College

FEB 1 1 2014

This book is dedicated
to John & Dixie Woodard, my mom and dad…
being their son is the best internship I'll ever have.

CONTENTS

INTERNSHIP:

Agreement where a student works for an employer in exchange for access to special knowledge and people.

66 You are about to
embark upon the
Great Crusade,
toward which we
have striven these
many months. The
eyes of the world
are upon you. 99

IKE EISENHOWER

INTRODUCTION

Are you about to take that great leap of faith between school and work? If so, listen up.

Chances are, you're bursting at the seams to take that leap, but you're not sure where you'll land. It feels like you should be ready for this moment, but you wonder, "Am I prepared?" As you approach the academic finish line, it seems like you've done more than enough to earn the world's respect without question. But, are you getting the respect you feel you deserve? When you go out into the world to find work, will you land on your feet?

One in five…that's how many people under 30 are out of work right now. If you're under 25, it's more like one in four. Those numbers are pretty daunting if you're a young person headed into the workplace. Even more, if you've spent zillions of dollars to go to school and are in debt up to your eyeballs, you could be asking yourself, "OMG! Was this all worth it?!? How am I ever going to repay all this money back!?"

Don't panic. It was all worth it. However, I'm afraid I have some bad news for you. To excel in today's competitive work world, all those years in the classroom alone aren't enough. You need something more.

Most young people leaping into today's job market lack two things: skills and access. You need both, or you are sunk. How do you get the right skills and access? You get an internship, and you crush it. That is what this book is all about.

Being the clueless new person on the first day of the job has a long tradition. In the past, it has been understood that most people really don't know what the hell they are doing on their first day. However, those days are now over.

The stakes are higher now. For most employers the luxury of the long on-the-job learning curve is now too expensive. Today's employers need workers who are ready to go out of the box. In this case, the box is school. An internship can give you the edge.

In this book, I'll show you how to get the internship you want and how to be a fantastic intern once you do. *I'll reveal secrets that most internship supervisors never talk about, and I'll teach you tricks about the workplace that nobody ever learns in school.* The cool stuff I offer here is based on years as both an intern and an intern supervisor. This information is candid, powerful and unique; you won't find it anyplace else.

In 1997, I landed an internship at the White House, and within a year, I was able to turn that opportunity into a full-time job. Since then I've supervised hundreds of students pursuing internships with some of the most competitive programs in the country. Through trial and error, and lots of hard work, it's taken me over a decade to put together many of the internship lessons I offer in this book.

Whether you're trying to find an internship, about to start your first internship, or mid-way through your tenth internship, I guarantee that this information will help you by leaps and bounds.

Many of the ideas discuss are practical, actionable steps you can take that will not only make you stand out from the crowd, but will also earn your colleagues' respect. Let me show you a path to being a highly successful, extremely hirable intern that is easy, and possible to start NOW.

If you need convincing, in Part I of this book I'll talk about why you ought to pursue an internship. In Part II, I'll reveal some of my best techniques for landing a great internship. Part III will address what you should expect from an internship, and the attitude that almost all successful interns share. Part IV of this book covers the office skills every intern needs, but nobody ever takes the time to teach. In Part V, I'll give you a ton of office communication secrets that are vital for any intern's success in the workplace. Part VI offers my very best secrets about not just how to succeed, but how to crush it with your internship.

The books I like to read the most are by authors who write the way they talk. I have done my best to write this book that way. My focus is not to create high literature but to give you useful, actionable information.

Admittedly, I haven't included a ton of statistics here. Rather, the tips I offer here are largely based on my own expertise and firsthand experience. These techniques worked for me; they will work for you.

In this book, I have tried to avoid delving into the debate about the ethics of experiential learning, or the state of internships as an industry.

My sole focus here is to give you techniques that will help you be a great intern.

Are you ready to do that? If so, let's go.

PART ONE

Internship:
Why You Want One

Step 1:
Understand That They Don't
Tell You Everything In School

Step 2:
Learn The Basics
Before You Begin

Step 3:
Be Great On Day One

> " Ready are you?
> What know you
> of ready? "

YODA

Understand That They Don't Teach You Everything In School

You don't have a clue. Sorry, I know that sounds harsh – but if you're currently in school or just out of school, it's true. Why are you clueless? *Because they don't teach you everything in school.*

On your first day of school, before you got into the heavy stuff (counting, right hand/left hand, naptime, etc.), I bet your teacher spent some time teaching you how to learn, right? I know that's how it was for me.

My kindergarten teacher was awesome. The first day of school was scary, but Mrs. Guy took the time to make sure everybody knew where to go, what the rules were, and that everybody in the class was special. All through that first year I learned how to keep my stuff together, how to treat my classmates, and countless other things about how thrive in the classroom. All that stuff worked great for about the next 16 years.

But then, something happened to me and, if it hasn't already, it will happen to you too. I left the classroom. Oops.

Don't get me wrong – I have the greatest respect for formal education. I believe the greatest people in history have been teachers. Both my parents are teachers, and some of my greatest mentors in life were my teachers. There is nobody better than a great teacher and nobody worse than a bad one.

You may have heard the saying "teachers teach, others do." Whoever came up with that was an idiot. Teachers teach so others CAN do. It's one of the most worthy, selfless, impactful occupations there is. I'm not trying to diss teachers here. What I am saying, however, is that students coming out of schools today need to know more about real work than they do. There are some things they just don't teach you in school, but they should.

It is unbelievable to me how much time, money, and care we put into educating young people so they will be prepared for the real world. But then, we spend almost NO time teaching students about real life work. It leaves them feeling like smacking themselves in the forehead and saying, "I shoulda had a V8!"

Most who walk down the commencement aisle (high school, and especially college) feel ready to take on the world! Did you feel that way? I know I did. But during school, how many courses were you required to take called "how to find work" or "how to choose a profession"? How many lectures did you attend regarding what you should expect or how to act in the workplace? My guess: not too many.

That's a tragedy because *students entering the workplace today are some of the most skilled, energetic, and talented in history*. Newly-minted "grown-ups" today have more opportunities to reach their full potential than ever before!

Kate is a promising young woman I know who, after four years of tremendous dedication and hard work, is about to graduate from college. Once she takes that final exam and turns in that final paper, she's not sure exactly what she'll do. But she has over $75,000 in student debt and even though her parents are incredibly supportive, she feels a lot of pressure to find a job. In fact, to her, almost any job would do.

After all that time in school, Kate is just bursting to be a full-fledged grown-up, to be independent, to meet expectations, and to be respected. Kate knows all her hard work is supposed to pay off somehow – people have been assuring her of this her whole life – but she's just not sure how, and nobody has really explained it to her. I know so many students who are in the exact same boat as Kate.

Have you ever known somebody who was a professional student? It's understandable why some take refuge in school. After all the time the average student spends in school, it's comfortable, it's known – most of us get to be pretty good at school.

To be fair, I'm not the only one to recognize the need for students to know more about the workplace before they leave the classroom. Plenty of schools encourage their students to get internships – which is a great! But they get the transition all wrong.

> **66** Our species needs
> and deserves a
> citizenry with
> minds awake and a
> basic understanding
> of how the
> world works. **99**

CARL SAGAN

Learn The Basics
Before You Begin

Several years ago, Nick was assigned to be my intern. Nick had just completed his sophomore year at an Ivy League school, and I could tell from the beginning that he was incredibly smart (definitely smarter than me) and superbly well-intentioned. However, he didn't have a clue about work and it showed.

In part as a warm-up, and also because I needed it, I asked Nick if he would please make a single copy of a one page document. After 45 minutes, poor Nick returned, head down, with my single page original now slightly crumpled in his hand.

I asked, "Nick! What's the matter?" Nick said, "I couldn't do it." "Couldn't do what?" I asked. He replied, "I couldn't make the copy."

Some People Won't Like This Very Much

In my experience, there is almost always an inversely proportional relationship between the how good an intern is and the level of prestige associated with the school they attend. In other words, a lot of time the student from the University of Michigan is a better intern than the student from Harvard.

Now, this is a generalization. Have I had fantastic interns from Harvard and sucky interns from Michigan? You bet. But, I've had more good ones from Michigan. The point: when it comes to internships, don't fret about whether you attend a well-known school. A lot of internship supervisors are actually a little bit biased against the fancy schools.

If you're an Ivy Leaguer, well – I bet you're smart enough to figure out how to overcome those biases on your own.

This story might sound crazy – but when was the last time you used a photocopier? Would you recognize the buttons, know how to clear a paper jam, or refill paper on an unfamiliar machine?

Now, you might be saying, "Eric! I don't need to know how to make copies; I'm way more advanced than that!" Well, speaking from personal experience, the only thing I can say to you my friend is that when there is nobody else around and your big boss turns to you and says, "Would you mind please making four copies of this double sided and stapled?" you damn well better know how to do it – accurately and FAST. While you're at it, don't let the bead of sweat dripping off your brow hit the paper.

Nick studied Shakespeare, organic chemistry, calculus, and had 3.9 GPA. But he became paralyzed by a photocopier because he didn't know a few simple things. He was a product of state-of-the-art education, but nobody had taken the time to teach him even the most basic things about the workplace.

At this point, you might be saying, "But Eric! Isn't that what an internship is for? Isn't an internship SUPPOSED to be the place where you learn basic office skills?"

That might be true. You could spend your ENTIRE internship, working for free, learning about basic workplace skills through osmosis. But I think you can do better than that. I can guarantee that the people you're competing against for that one full-time staff opening plan to do better than that.

If you're spending your entire internship learning basic office skills, you're not going to have much time to focus on the unique

Think That Stint at McDonald's Taught You Nothing?

Think again. A lot of times the most menial, seemingly meaningless jobs you take as a student can teach you a lot skills that you'll use later in the workplace. When a restaurant manager tells you to refill the soda machine and there is a crowd of thirsty people who want a drink, you somehow figure it out. Because, if you don't, that thirsty mob might just kill you.

Don't seek out a job that makes you empty trash cans. But, if that's what you wind up with when you're starting out, realize it may not be a total loss. Pick up what skills you can doing grunt work and you'll have an edge over your peers who have no experience getting their hands dirty in the real world.

skills, people, or opportunities you should. So don't. Get a handle on the basic stuff ahead of time.

" I need a hero. "

BONNIE TYLER

Be Great On Day One

L et me put it this way, if you show up on day one of your internship and you already have the basic stuff down, you're going to have a HUGE advantage over your peers. *Make no mistake, when it comes to internships, first impressions are a big deal.* When a staffer knows they are going to have to work with an intern for the next however many months, they are just looking for any clue they can find to figure out who the best interns might be.

That first impression will likely determine where you'll work, when you'll work, who you'll be working with, what you'll be doing, and how you'll be doing it. Remember when you got picked for a reading or math group in school and how that kind of tracked you for the rest of your days? That first impression you give during your internship is a little bit like that.

Does Someone Have The Wrong Impression?

If, for whatever reason, you wind up working with somebody (another intern, a staffer) during your internship that has the wrong impression about you, change it. If they take an action or make a comment that implies something about you that is untrue, call them on it.

For example, suppose somebody has the impression that you are anti-social and they invite everybody but you to an after work thing that you would actually like to be a part of. Simply ask them in a nice way, "Why do you think I wouldn't like to come?" Interrupt their assumptions about you. Don't wait to do it, do it early on. The longer false assumptions remain unchallenged, the deeper they sink in.

I recall a time when a new group of interns arrived on a day when I happened to be out of the office. When the new group walked around to meet everybody in the office, I missed it. The next day one of these new interns, Michelle, took it upon herself to come find me so she could introduce herself. Bravo – great initiative…way to stand out from the crowd!

Except in Michelle's case, she wound up shuffling in my office slurping on an iced coffee through a straw. She didn't have a pen, she didn't have paper, she didn't have a card…just coffee - for herself, not me - which she continued to slurp. Not a good first impression.

Imagine instead if Michelle has stepped forward with pen and paper in hand, ready to take notes about any cool projects I happened to need help with. What if she had her contact info all ready to hand over? What if she had given off the vibe that she was ready to work rather than…don't give me anything to do, I'm sipping Starbucks?

I've seen it countless times. A new group of interns arrives, but there are some who stand out on the first day because they are more focused, more confident. Over the years, I've supervised hundreds of interns. Some I remember, some I don't. A lot of the ones I remember are now colleagues, because they got hired.

Are you worried that you've already started out on the wrong foot? Don't worry. Just like the reading or math group in school, it's possible to jump onto a better track – it just takes a little more work. Keep reading.

PART TWO

How To Get An Internship

66

We shall
find a way,
or make one.

99

HANNIBAL OF CARTHAGE

If I knew just a fraction of what I know now on the first day of my first internship, I can only imagine where I would be. But first, a little background…

I grew up as an expatriate kid in Bangkok, Thailand. My dad did community development training for the Thai government, and my mom taught at the International School of Bangkok, where I went to school. Bangkok was an AWESOME place to grow up, and my closest friends in the world are still the ones I made there.

By the time I graduated from high school, I knew a lot about the world, but not very much about living in the States. I looked and sounded American, but I'd never really lived in the U.S. American slang sometimes got the better of me.

I remember my first summer back in the U.S. – in Missouri – I got a part-time lifeguard job at a local swimming pool. Before reporting to work on the first day, I asked the pool supervisor over the phone if there was anything special I might need for the first day of work. She replied, "Just your swim trunks and plenty of elbow grease."

Assuming that "elbow grease" was some kind of special suntan lotion for lifeguards, I proceeded directly to the nearest Wal-Mart where I searched relentlessly up and down the aisles until finally a sales associate asked, "Young man, can I help you?" When I told her I was searching for "elbow grease" she looked at me like I was a mental patient. I was a little bit lost, to say the least.

As I headed off to my freshman year of college, my disorientation continued from there. Over the next four and a half years, I transferred colleges SEVEN TIMES. I wound up attending schools in Illinois, Missouri, Oklahoma, Hawaii, and Guam. Finding a college where I could fit in was a real struggle for me. I had moved around so much; it was really hard to know where I belonged.

After all that, I was frazzled. I felt like I needed to get away from it all. So, I packed up my gear and headed back to Guam to be a SCUBA instructor. This was about as far away from the typical office setting as you can imagine. In fact, I remember flying into Guam a flight attendant remarked to me how beautiful the water looked from the air. I explained to her with a smile, "I know. That's my office." I went from school, to a school of fish.

I wound up diving on Guam for the next three years. My hair grew out into this giant sun bleached crown of curls, and I rarely wore shoes. I literally spent thousands of hours underwater with the fish and the octopuses and the puffer fish and the turtles. It wound up being thousands of hours of therapy.

By the time I was 24, I started to get my bearings. Getting through college had been so hard for me, I felt like I needed to do something to show for it. Spending hours under the sea was fun, but I was restless to use my brain. So, I thought to myself, "Where would be the most prestigious, respectable place I could work?" My answer: The White House.

I had always loved politics and (forgive me if my politics don't match yours) been a die-hard Democrat. But, as a salty dog on the sea, I had no idea how I might get to the White House. It was literally on the other side of the Earth. This was in the mid-90s, when the Internet was just starting to get off the ground. Information online was still scarce…and Guam was far, far way.

So, I sat down and wrote a letter. Something along the lines of "Dear White House, how can I come help out?" I slapped a stamp on it, put it in the mail, and figured I'd never hear back. But I was starting to get inspired. So, I sent off a bunch more letters to graduate schools asking for their application info. I figured that maybe something would come through.

Over the next couple of months, I started to get catalogs and application forms from all sorts of graduate schools. To my great shock, I also heard back from the White House. They sent me an official White House internship application in an official White House envelope. At that point, I had never really heard of such a thing as an internship, but it sounded pretty good to me.

Having transferred colleges so many times, one thing I did become very good at was filling out applications. So still in my "scuba-fied" state I started filling out a ton of applications to graduate schools and, on a whim, even sent in the application to the White House. I figured if nothing else came of it, I could still keep the cool White House envelope.

That spring, to my great surprise, I received an acceptance letter from the International Affairs program at George Washington University in

Landing in a New Place to Do Your Internship

You may be in a situation where in order to do an internship, you will need to travel to a new place. Sometimes, the work and extra costs associated with needing to set up shop in a new place discourages students from pursuing an internship in the first place. Do not let this happen to you.

Instead, realize that as a student intern, you don't need very many creature comforts to get by. Go into your internship like a Spartan. Maintain a mindset that you will be able to get by on very little. Plan to spend a lot of time at your internship – don't worry if the place you're staying isn't the most ideal. All you need is a place to sleep and a place to get ready in the morning. Maybe some place to do laundry, if you're lucky. Don't fret about not having a car – get by on public transportation if you can.

Be lean during your internship. Eliminate distractions. Focus on the internship.

Washington, DC. My first thought was, "I'm going to have to start wearing shoes again." After making some quick arrangements, a few short weeks later I landed in DC with a single backpack and the hope that being a grad student would be easier than being an undergraduate.

To my great relief, getting set up in DC wasn't nearly as hard as I thought it might be and after a few days of class I quickly made a bunch of great new friends. I started running around the monuments on the National Mall almost every morning. It was during one of these runs, as I went past the White House that I thought, "I should call those guys. They never even sent me a rejection letter." So I did.

I managed to get a hold of the White House internship coordinator. She asked, "Is this Eric Woodard?"

I said, "Yes, I was just wondering what happened with my application."

She asked, "Eric from Guam?"

I said, "Yes, from Guam – but I'm in DC now."

She said, "Eric! We've been trying to get in touch with you! Can you start your internship next week?"

I couldn't believe it.

So, one week later, there I was: an intern in the White House, assigned to the Office of the First Lady Hillary Rodham Clinton. I was more than wet behind the ears; I was a fish out of water.

How did I manage to land that internship? I didn't have any real political connections and wasn't a particularly accomplished student. By any conventional measure, there is no way I should have been able to pull it off.

I didn't realize it at the time, but I stumbled my way into the White House by doing a lot of things right without even knowing it. Maybe I had filled out so many applications over the years that I had some kind of subconscious mojo going on. Whatever the case might be, I now know that a lot of the conventional wisdom students hear about applying for internships (or fellowships, scholarships, jobs, and the like) is just dead wrong.

Imagine yourself in the shoes of someone tasked with going through hundreds of internship applications. What would you focus on? How would you feel? It is easy for me to imagine being in this position because, over the years, I've been in this exact situation many times. I've often imagined how my internship application seemed to the person reviewing it, and now know why I was pulled from the pile.

" Two roads
diverged in a
wood, and I – I
took the one less
traveled by, and
that has made all
the difference. "

ROBERT FROST

Stand Out Like A Sore Thumb

It wasn't my intention, but when I applied for my first internship at the White House I was such a weirdo at the time, I couldn't help but stand out from the crowd. A place like the White House receives hundreds of applications for its internship program, and they all look pretty much alike.

Basically, the average applicant is a college sophomore or junior attending a very prestigious if not Ivy League school. Chances are, they are attending a school someplace between North Carolina and Maine – there might be a few Californians or Michiganders in there – but most applicants are from the East Coast. As a dude who had transferred colleges seven times, and was now on Guam, I was about as far away from the mold as possible.

Often students will try to "stand out from the rest of the crowd" by seeming more accomplished than the rest. Surrounded by a group of highly qualified and motivated competitors, this is really hard to do. Being super amazing isn't that much better than being really amazing. *Instead of trying to be more amazing than the rest, just be different.*

Assume that the person going through that pile of applications is a bleary-eyed reviewer, just desperate for an excuse to pull any application from the stack. As a reviewer of applications, I've actually caught myself shouting out loud, "Good Lord! Please, just say something, anything that is different!", because all of the applications look the same. If you can, make the actual physical application different. Print it out on some crazy colored paper or print it sideways – anything that is different.

Include a cover letter with your application, even if they don't ask for one. When you do, it communicates a bunch of messages to your application reviewer. It indicates that you are willing to do extra work. It says you care enough about this opportunity to do extra. Including a cover letter suggests you have initiative and are prone to over-deliver. An unsolicited cover letter indicates that you are polished, and take pride in your work. Including a cover letter when one isn't required indicates that you are able to think outside the box – that you can think beyond simple instructions. When you have a cover letter and most other applications don't, you will stand out. As Alison Green writes in her blog www.askamanager.org, there are "two reasons your cover letter sucks: 1. It doesn't exist. You just sent your resume. Adding a three-sentence note in the mail doesn't count. 2. It exists, but it might as well not, because it just repeats the same info that's on your resume." *Don't let your cover letter suck.*

Another great way to stand out has to do with when you apply. Consider the point of view of somebody accepting applications. If an application deadline runs from February 1 to March 15, the reviewer is going to assume that the vast majority of applications are going to arrive on March 14 or even March 15. *What if you are the applicant who sends in their application on February 2?*

For somebody accepting applications, they are going to notice the application that arrives on February 2. If for no other reason, they will be glad to get your application because it's a sign that somebody out there is interested in the opportunity they have to offer. Moreover, there is a good chance yours is the only application the reviewer is going to have for a while. This means that your application has a captive audience for all that time. Think that can make a difference? You bet it will.

" **I'm kind of a big deal.** "

RON BURGUNDY

Want My References?
Go To Hell

Resumes, my God, resumes – they are an art unto themselves. Everybody has a strong opinion about resumes; here I can only offer my own advice.

Before I do, let me stipulate my intransigent belief that a resume must be your own. *In the end, no matter how much advice you get from how many people, the most important thing about your resume is that it's genuine and speaks about who you truly are.* If a resume isn't genuine, it will be obvious to any reviewer. It's easy to spot a fake resume from miles away.

The mistake most people make with their resume is that they make it look like every other resume. So often, all resumes look the same! If you are going to send in a resume (and I stress IF – because you should not assume you must send in the traditional resume), please do everything you can to make it stand out.

The resume I sent into the White House was printed in color (very rare in 1997) and had a scanned photo of me embedded into the document. If I had to do it over I would have sent it in printed on eggroll wrappers or something – the more different, the better. Being different feels risky, but it's not. As Seth Godin says (and if you haven't read any of his stuff, do), *"Being risky is safe, and being safe is risky."*

It never ceases to amaze me how so many internship applicants will try to hide that they are different. If you represent a minority group (ethnic, geographic, sexual orientation, whatever), let that come through on your resume! Don't hold back! Please beat the reviewer over the head with it. Most programs are always on the look for diversity, and if they're not, you don't want to intern there anyway. *Being unique makes you scarce and being scarce makes you valuable.*

In most contexts, especially with internship applications, a resume has one purpose: to get the attention of a reviewer so you get pulled from the pile for an interview, or whatever the next step is in the process.

When you send a resume electronically (as most resumes now travel), make sure it is one file, and that the file is your name (i.e. EricWoodard. doc, EricWoodard.pdf). In other words, you want to avoid file names like EricResume#15.doc. Send it as a Word or Adobe file. If the application doesn't specify, Word is probably safer. If you are sending your resume with other documents as part of an application, send it all as one file. Scan it and send as an Adobe file if you need to. *Send it whichever way is going to make it easiest for the receiver to handle it, open it, and read it.*

You can assume that a reviewer will be looking at your resume for about 10 seconds...maybe 15. If you don't catch their attention in that time, you're toast.

This means, for goodness sake, your resume should be one page. Think you are too accomplished to fit everything on one page? I've seen Members of Congress and Nobel Prize winners who are in their 70s who can get it all on one page. You can too.

See all that white space around the border and within the text of your resume? That's resume real-estate you're not using: one page.

When you list your address on your resume, be mindful of the message that address conveys. If you list a "school" address and a "home" address...that really screams college student. If you're applying for an internship in New York City but you list a Newark address, it raises the question, "Is this person available? Are they going to try and commute?" On the other hand, if you're applying to work for a Member of Congress from Montana – you'd better list a Montana address if there is any way you truthfully can.

Put an email address on there that isn't crazy. In high school I did a lot of really cool bird and duck imitations (which are still awesome). For the longest time, I sported the email address bird12@. In hindsight, that probably didn't make me seem too professional , but back then email was still kind of new-fangled thing anyway...so maybe it was okay. But it's definitely NOT okay today. If you don't already have one, get a professional sounding email address that is some version of your name. Pick one you like because as soon as you start giving it out, that will be the address you

Is Your Resume Lazy?

Don't be afraid to tweak your resume for every internship/job application you put together. Fine tune a resume so that it focuses on how you can add value to wherever you are applying. In fact, if you can, re-do your resume for every new opportunity. Tailor it to the opportunity at hand. Is that more work? Yes. Does that mean you need to be really careful about catching typos and formatting issues because you're creating a new document each time? Yes. Will your resume help you stand out as somebody particularly well suited for a position? Absolutely.

If you have a choice between sending in a few applications that are really good vs. applying to a ton of internships with applications that are kind of blah – always go quality, not quantity. Go deep on fewer applications rather than go wide on many. You want your resume to be the best one in the stack. If it's not, you're toast.

use to start building your professional network.

The state-of-the-art resume has your contact info at the top followed by three sections going down the page: 1) Education, 2) Experience, and 3) Special Skills/Interests. Under each of those sections, list stuff you have done in reverse chronological order. Put some relevant bullet points under each.

But again, your resume doesn't have to follow the conventional format – don't be afraid to stand out. *In the end, a resume is just a business card; it's just a way to get attention. Use it like that.*

Lastly, in the name of Pete and all that is holy, *PLEASE don't put "references available upon request" at the bottom of your resume!*

Let me ask you, if you're applying for an internship, and the application reviewer calls and says, "Hey...I really like your application...but let me ask you...do you have any references I might contact?" Are you going to reply, "Oh my God! I can't believe you asked me that! Although you've made the request, there is no way I'm going to give you my references. Screw you, man!!"

" Don't try to be
perfect; just be an
excellent example of
being human. **,**

TONY ROBBINS

Tell A Story, Be A Human

My White House internship application required essay answers to two questions. I recall that my answer to the first question addressed my philosophy about the role of government; the second talked about my story under the ocean all the way out in Guam. I guarantee that the second essay was the one that helped me get accepted.

I can't tell you how many times I've looked at a stack of applications from a group of similar applicants and have needed to do a double take regarding the essays they've submitted because they were all the same. Not too long ago, I was reviewing answers to the question "What has been your greatest learning experience?" Ninety percent of the applicants talked about graduate school as being their most important learning experience. Is there anything wrong with that answer? No. Is it possible that happens to be the truth for those people who answered that way? Sure. Is it particularly attention grabbing? No.

Among that group I remember one applicant who stood out by describing the bike ride he took that morning. It was different, and way more interesting. His was the one I pulled from the pile. *I just needed an excuse to pull one application, and that essay was all I needed.*

Maggie was an intern who worked for me years ago who I remember very well not only because she was a terrific intern, but also because her intern application told a crazy story. You may not have a story like Maggie – but if you do, use it! I can't remember what the question was, but Maggie's essay described how she had been in a terrible car accident that resulted in her arm being "severed." Think that application stood out? You're damn right it did. Maggie got accepted in about two microseconds.

The thing was, when Maggie showed up for her first day of her internship, she had two arms! When I asked her what happened, she explained that her arm had actually been only partially severed, and that doctors had been able to re-attach it so she had almost full use of her arm. I knew she was telling the truth because she still sported a big bandage. I was glad Maggie kept her arm; she had a great story and turned out to be a spectacular intern.

Now you might be saying, "But Eric! I don't have a story that makes me look good." If that's true for you, then it is all the better. In fact, I think you're much better off telling a story that describes a failure. Why? *Because everybody can relate to struggle, everybody can relate to failing.* When somebody writes about all their great success they've had, it's not so interesting. Do you have a story about how you've failed, messed up, were arrested, been beaten down, but are still standing? If so, you may have a blockbuster on your hands.

As you put together your application, if you can't bring yourself to reveal your life's struggles, at least make sure you reveal that you are a human. If you're a runner, make sure it shows up someplace in your application. If you do scrap-booking, talk about it! You never know, the person reading your application may be a scrap-booker too. Unless you're applying to a very exotic internship program, you are almost guaranteed that the application reviewer is human, so make sure it comes across that you are too.

The people deciding whether or not to accept you as an intern are interested in knowing whether you are the sort of person they can tolerate in the workplace. Staffers want reassurance that they can survive co-existence with you, and ideally, might even enjoy hanging out with you. A lot of things about the workplace are

So You're A Recovering Drug Addict Who Spent Time In Jail For Clubbing Baby Seals...

Do you have some crazy failure or lapse in judgment in your past that you're embarrassed about? Are you worried that failure will keep you from getting an internship? Feel like you need to hide it? Don't.

Instead, embrace that crazy thing from your past. In fact, bring it up yourself. Put it out there all raw and human for the reviewer of your internship application to see. Is it possible that your checkered past will scare the reviewer off? It's possible.

However, I think the greater danger is that a reviewer will dismiss you because you're boring. If your internship application stands out because you're willing to show your flaws, warts and all – at least it's going to be interesting. More than that, telling the ugly truth conveys to the reviewer that you learn from mistakes and have some real life experience. It will show the reviewer that you're not afraid to tell the truth and that more than anything, you're not afraid to show who you are – that you are authentic.

inhuman enough already, make sure you don't come across as a droid through your internship application.

I remember one occasion where I was left with two candidates to fill one internship slot. It was a really close call. I re-read both applications, and noticed that Tom listed how he played trumpet, while the other candidate did not. Tom seemed more human, so he got the internship. He turned out to be a heck of nice guy, and I still remember him as one of the best interns I've ever worked with.

66 You don't carry
in your
countenance
a letter of **99**
recommendation.

CHARLES DICKENS

Recommendation Letters

A lot of people treat letters of recommendation like they are state secrets…and this drives me absolutely nuts.

Before computers were mainstream and email was so groovy, when I applied to college I had to ask people to seal letters in an envelope and sign the back – like the signature was some sort of unbreakable seal. I don't think this is as prevalent as it used to be, but some folks still rely on this medieval requirement.

I swear, it would be easier to get a Somali pirate to write a fake letter of recommendation, stick it in an envelope with their signature across the back, and mail it anywhere in the world than it would be to get a bona fide academic teacher to provide a real letter. I don't know where people get the signature across the back thing. Is it to make the letter author feel like they can write candidly?

I've got to tell you, if somebody doesn't have the backbone to tell a student what they really think about the student's performance, they're probably not a very good teacher and therefore, their judgment forming the basis of the letter probably isn't worth much.

As you go through school or as you have bosses or internship supervisors you think would speak highly of you, ask them for a generic letter of recommendation addressed, "To Whom It May Concern." If you need to, offer to draft a letter for them. Also ,(this is important) ask for these letters while you're still seeing them on an everyday basis. Teachers and internship supervisors see a lot of students. You want them to write the letter for you while you are still front and center in their mind.

Once you have a collection of these letters, you'll never need to worry about asking for a letter from the biology professor you had 6 years ago. If you're applying someplace that requires a letter writer to send the letter directly, just print out a copy and send it to the letter author with an addressed stamped envelope and a nice note requesting that they seal the letter and drop it in the mail.

Increasingly, people are writing letters of recommendation by email. Whenever you can, ask the people who write your letters of recommendation to stick their words on letterhead. People, especially people who review internship applications, are conditioned to scan email. If your letter of recommendation comes to them as an email, it might not get the attention it deserves just because it looks like an email.

What Have You Done for Me Lately?

I can't tell you how many students make this mistake when applying for internships, but A LOT do. They fill out their internship applications from the standpoint of, "I would be great candidate for this internship program because your internship matches my career goals and will help me pursue my dreams."

When I read applications like that, my inner monologue response is, "Well, Beatrice (pretend the applicant is named Beatrice), that's all fine and good, but how does that help me and my organization?"

Don't get me wrong; internships are a two-way street, where students trade work for experience from an employer. However, the application isn't necessarily the best place to highlight the part of the deal that benefits you. Instead, why not fill out your internship application with your emphasis on the part that will benefit your employer? In other words, approach it like this: "I would be a great candidate for this internship program because I know all about your organization, and can offer you lots of skills and abilities that will help your organization achieve its goals."

See the difference?

" Rules are not
necessarily sacred,
principles are. **"**

FRANKLIN DELEANOR ROOSEVELT

Break The Rules, But Only The Big Ones

Like I've said, you want to be DIFFERENT – so that means you're going to have to break the rules a little bit with your application.

If they ask for three references, then send them three references along with five letters of recommendation, or five videos with people singing your praises. *Send a cover letter, always, even if they don't ask for one.* Have your application bound. Take a look at what you're about to send in and ask, "How can I make this more awesome?"

If you are worried that the application reviewer will think that you missed the instructions, just state something like, "I know you asked for this, but I thought it might be helpful if I gave you more." This shows that you have initiative, are prone to over deliver, and can predict a supervisor's needs. People reviewing internship applications are begging to see this stuff.

After years of school, most students are conditioned to ask for permission to do pretty much anything. When it comes to applying for that dream internship however, you can't afford to ask for permission. I guarantee your strongest competitors won't. If the internship application doesn't call for something that you know makes you look good – send it in anyway!

In that same spirit, don't get rattled or scared away by some requirement you don't quite meet. For example, let's say you've just finished school but want to apply for an internship that requires applicants to be "current students." Apply anyway. If you need to, go take a weekend course on pottery (congratulations, now you're a student). See what I mean? Chances are the person reviewing your internship application didn't write it and likely doesn't know or care what the requirements are to begin with. They are most concerned with finding good interns. Don't let the big things get in your way.

On the other hand, make sure you sweat the little details. This means, for God's sake, no spelling errors in your application. I can't tell you how many students have addressed applications to me as "Dear Mr. Woodward." Make sure the formatting is consistent. Don't change fonts or styles half way through. Don't be sloppy. Remember, the application reviewer is just looking for an excuse to pull your application out of the pile but they are also looking for an excuse to send your application to the reject pile.

66

Do not run a
campaign that
would embarrass
your mother.

99

Robert Byrd

Make Your Internship Application Like A Campaign

Most students send in their internship application and think "That's it, that's all I can do." Wrong! You should treat your internship application effort like a campaign.

Think about when you are applying for your internship. If you have the flexibility, consider applying for the spring or fall. Most programs are bombarded with applications in the summer, but are desperate for interns in the spring and fall. *If you can offer yourself during a time when most students are unavailable, especially May and August, do.* Most students can't offer themselves to work full time. If you can figure out a way to be full time, be sure to pitch yourself that way.

Before you even apply, you should do some research about your target organization. Get online and find out what they do and what they are interested in. Know anybody currently working at that organization?

Talk to them. Ask, "What are they looking for in potential interns?" This seems obvious, but most folks forget to take this simple step. Let the competition's laziness be your advantage.

If you don't know anybody within the organization, still, call them up cold. Ask to speak to the intern coordinator, introduce yourself. Let them know, "I'm about to apply to your internship program, I've researched all about your organization (make sure you have), and I've read the application information (make sure you have), but I was wondering if I could ask what the most important thing you are looking for in potential interns." Unless they actually have a sentence in their application materials that says "The most important thing we seek in our interns is…", you're asking a valid question.

If you can't get to the internship coordinator, ask the same questions of whoever you can get on the phone. Chances are, they work with lots of interns at that organization, or they might even be an intern themselves. If you do get the intern coordinator on the phone, make sure to follow up with a note (ideally, an actual physical note) thanking them for taking the time to talk with you. This is before you've even applied.

When you do apply (remember to over-deliver on the application), be strategic about how you send it. If they ask for it to be emailed, make sure you send it as one clean attachment with your name as the file name. When you are compared against others who send in their information with a bunch of haphazardly named random attachments, this makes you look good.

Don't be afraid to also send in a hard copy of your application, and when you do, send it in a Priority Mail envelope so it stands out. Avoid FedEx or UPS – that can result in somebody having to make a trip downstairs to get your application from a courier – not good. Stick a note in there with an explanation about why you're sending a hard copy. Something like, "I'm sending you a hard copy because I know you already have enough of these to print out and wanted to save you the trouble of printing mine." Or, "I'm sending you a hard copy because I wanted to

All's Fair in Love, War, and Internships

During the internship application process, some students get all hung up on inconsiderate behavior by a potential employer.

The thinking starts to follow this pattern: "I'm jumping through all these hoops to show them what a fantastic intern I would be, and they won't even return my calls! Screw `em." Or, it's something like "I'm amazingly talented, if they don't recognize how amazing I am and aren't begging me to be their intern…screw `em!" Yes, it's a lot like dating.

That line of reasoning isn't necessarily wrong, but if your purpose is to get the internship and access to the people and skills that come with it, I'm not sure how far your focusing on the unfairness of the process will get you.

Fairness is one of those things that most students don't learn enough about when they are in school. In school, things are always supposed to be fair. In the working world, I'm sorry to be the one to tell you, things are very rarely fair.

Is it fair that you may have to jump through a bunch of hoops just to be considered for an internship? Nope. Is it reality? Yes. The sooner you understand that things in the working world aren't always fair, the sooner you'll be able to thrive in that world. You don't have to perpetuate unfairness, but you need to understand it.

include this (portfolio, recording, DVD, that one awesome thing that makes you look good etc.).

Sometimes employers will want to interview perspective interns. If you get called in for an interview, this is actually a good thing because it gives you an even greater opportunity to be different from the rest.

Follow all the normal job interviewing rules. When I go to an interview, I get myself to the front door about 30 minutes early. Then, I go find a nice quiet place to calm down for the next 20 minutes to cool off and collect my thoughts. This lets me time my arrival to the actually reception area about 5 minutes ahead of the interview. Dress sharp, and turn off your cell phone.

If you do this one thing during the interview, you will be miles ahead of your competition: take notes. Most students in the workplace don't know to do this – but it's hugely important. Some might ask, "why should I take notes, I don't even work here yet." I reply, "with that attitude, you never will." On the other hand, if I'm interviewing you, and you think what I have to say is important enough to take notes on BEFORE you even work for me, then I'm going to want to see what you can do when you're interning for real.

Also, before you go into the interview, have a thank you note ready to go (addressed envelope, stamp, etc.). Complete the short note after the interview, including any pertinent details so it's sincere. Then mail it within an hour or so of finishing the interview. If you can do it without risking an awkward situation, come back to that office and hand deliver the note (don't worry that the stamp isn't cancelled – that will just draw more attention to your note).

After you send in an internship application, if enough time has passed that you worry they've forgotten about you – don't be shy, call them. There are hundreds of reasons you might not have heard from a perspective internship supervisor. Maybe they lost your number, maybe your acceptance letter got stuck in the mail, maybe your dog ate it, maybe their server is funky and their message went in your spam folder, maybe they are just busy and need you to call so they can just offer you the position on the spot. I often think, when I applied to the White House, what if I'd never called to follow up? What an opportunity I would have missed!

If, after all this, you get word that your application has been rejected, you're still not finished. *Most people miss this next step.* Call whoever reviewed your application and ask them for feedback. Ask them specifically how your application could be improved, and what turned them off. You may find that your application was awesome – that there were just other circumstances at play. Or, you may get some really valuable feedback that will help you next time round.

Even after you've received the rejection – if it's an internship you really want – follow up with the intern coordinator one last time. Send them one more thing, a piece of writing, an article, something you've created, with a short note along the lines of, "Dear intern coordinator – just wanted to thank you again for reviewing my application. On the off chance that you've had a slot open up, I just wanted to share this [insert the thing that makes you look awesome] so you can see that I would be really qualified to fill your opening."

Do you think this is overkill? Tam didn't. Tam applied to a summer internship program I managed many years ago for Senator Clinton. I really wanted to accept Tam. But, for various reasons, I just didn't have the slot to offer him. While rejection letters started to go out, I even made up a fake "wait list" category for Tam in the hope that I might find a solution. In the end however, I had to call Tam and explain we just couldn't take him. At that point, most students might have thrown in the towel, but not Tam.

A few days later the front office called to let me know that someone had dropped off an envelope for me. It turned out to be a thank you note from Tam with just one more writing sample to show how awesome he was. I decided that we needed to accept Tam on the spot. A few months later, Tam was hired as a full-time staffer. Several years later, Tam became Sen. Clinton's intern coordinator. Besides being awesome, Tam never gave up, and it really paid off.

If You Need To, Guilt Them Into It

Suppose you hit the end of the road. The internship supervisor has given you a final "no." Short of becoming a stalker, there are three more things you can do. First, give the reviewer one final thank you. Second, let them know that if they wind up losing an intern mid-term, you stand ready to step in. Third, let them know that you fully intend to apply for the next internship session.

If you're lucky, the internship supervisor will get your earnest message right around the time some of the interns that were chosen are acting particularly entitled and goofy. When the internship supervisor compares your attitude with the attitude of other students who were accepted – they may feel so guilty that they will just tell you to come in.

PART THREE

What To Expect From Your Internship

Step #10:
Don't Get Rattled By
THE GLARE

Step #11:
Know The Bright Line

Step #12:
You're The FNG

Step #13:
Tune In

Step #14:
Show Your ID

Step #15:
Shield Your
Magnetic Personality

Step #16:
Find A Place To Dwell

> **"** Wisdom is not a
> product of
> schooling but the
> lifelong attempt to
> acquire it. **"**

ALBERT EINSTEIN

Step #17:
Show Up And Be Present

Step #18:
Prevent, Predict, Problem Solve

Step #19:
Manage Your Manager

Step #20:
Slay Dragons

Step #21:
Shun And Lead The Herd

Step #22:
The Last Suit You'll Ever Wear

Step #23:
Everybody Is Human

66 Son I've lived a
life, of reading
people's faces,
knowing what the
cards are, by the
way they've held
their eyes. Now if
you don't mind me
saying, I can see
you're out of aces.
For a taste of your
whiskey, I'll give
you some advice. 99

KENNY ROGERS

Don't Get Rattled By
THE GLARE

For whatever reason, nobody tells bright-eyed, world changing, young professionals such as you the truth. Which is…*as a young person in the workplace, especially as an intern, you have to watch out for the GLARE!*

What is the GLARE? It's the silent look a battle-hardened, 20 year workplace veteran gives a first-day intern when the intern says something that shows their youth and professional inexperience. The GLARE is a look that says, "My God, child, you are so naïve and clueless." The GLARE says, "Young man/lady, you are going to have to EARN every ounce of respect you get from me." The GLARE says, "Grrrrrrrrrrrrr." Sound harsh? It is.

I'm sorry to be the one to have to tell you about the GLARE. It's a secret that everybody has been keeping from you. We keep it from all the young people. After enough scrapes and bruises in the workplace, most people learn about the GLARE the hard way, on their own. Believe it or not, I consider myself a glass-is-half-full personality – an optimist – and it's hard for me to be such a downer. I just want you to understand that the work world is a very different place from the school world.

However, the good news is that if you understand some of the differences between work and school going in, you will be ready to avoid the GLARE, or handle it when it happens. If you know what to expect from your internship, if you have the right skills, the right attitude, and know how to communicate effectively, you can jump across many workplace pitfalls like an intern ninja.

" I was a loner as a child. I had an imaginary friend – I didn't bother with him. **"**

GEORGE CARLIN

Know The Bright Line

Aristotle said, "Man is a social animal." I agree. In school (if your experience was anything like mine), there were a few loners, bullies, introverts, etc., but, generally, it's safe to assume that most people are out to make friends of one kind or another. However it's important to understand that at work, this isn't always the case.

Typically, a new intern fresh out of the classroom approaches work with the logical assumption that everybody is interested in being friends: other interns, staff, their boss, etc. This might be true, but not always.

Modern workers often spend more time with their coworkers than their family members. Understand that some office dwellers draw a very specific line between their work relationships and their personal relationships because they want to make sure that the former never threaten the latter.

Is this okay? You bet it is. *People are paid to be at work to do work, not make friends.* Do people work better with each other when they are friendly

The Hallway

I don't know if you'll experience this, but I remember that when I first started out as an intern the experience of passing people in the hallway was a little surreal.

When I just started out, I noticed that the way people passed each other in an office hallway was very different than a school hallway. Specifically, there seems to be a lot less smiling, nodding, and in general, acknowledgement of other human beings in the workplace hallway.

If close coworkers encounter each other in the office hallway, or people who have something to discuss bump into each other – things tend to be friendly. But otherwise, a lot of people maintain that thousand yard stare when they are on the move at work.

People at work tend to be focused, they tend to have things on their mind, and they tend to have things to do. As a new intern, if you feel like people are looking straight through you, don't worry. It's them, not you.

with each other? Yes, they do. But it's not necessarily a pre-requisite.

If you're a newbie in the workplace, it's important to understand that this has nothing to do with you – it's nothing personal. If somebody you work with doesn't show interest in being your friend, don't be offended.

In fact, if as a new intern you encounter a staffer (especially a supervisor) who seems overly friendly (especially compared to the behavior of others), you might want to maintain just a bit of caution. I've seen situations where staffers who have trouble getting along with colleagues decide they will build their social circle around each new group of interns. It goes without saying that this phenomenon can cause all sorts of trouble for an intern.

Be aware that any office you enter already has its own tangled web of personalities and internal politics. As an intern, you're there to learn and get access – the best way to do this is to stay above the fray. Especially when you first start out, don't worry about making close friendships with coworkers. *Instead, focus on building a reputation for being a good worker.* After you've been in the trenches long enough with colleagues, friendships will come through respect for your work. When you're first starting out, those are the kind of relationships you want at work.

In the workplace, people with a good sense of professionalism are reluctant to befriend people they are charged with supervising, especially when they haven't known each other for very long. After all, it is difficult to reprimand a friend. The best staff will often maintain a certain professional distance with more junior staff. Since, as an intern you will likely be the lowest person on the totem pole, be prepared for some cold shoulders when it comes to making friends at the office. Even if a boss or supervisor really wants to let their hair down and reach out, understand they might have reasons to hold back.

It's always fascinating to me to watch a boss' behavior on an employee's last day; I've seen this so many times. When it's time for the final goodbye, the boss who has been a little stiff and buttoned up for years with an employee will suddenly melt. You'll see smiles, hugs, effusive praise, even tears. The boss doesn't have to worry about managing that staffer any more. A supervisor who may have repressed a natural inclination toward friendliness for a long time is suddenly free to show their true feelings to their subordinate.

They don't teach this stuff in school. Most new interns haven't considered the aspect of making friends at work, but you should.

> " Where are you
> boys from in
> the world? "

LIEUTENANT DAN

STEP 12

You're The "FNG"

When I was on Guam, I often worked with Clubmates. These were young men and women from the U.S. mainland, mostly just out of college, who would rotate on and off the island for a six month stint working at a resort. During my years diving on Guam, I saw several generations of Clubmates come and go. It was a little like reality TV, and always interesting to watch people getting acclimated to island life between their first day and their last. New arrivals to the island were often lovingly referred to as "FNGs" (aka F$%^#$* New Guys) by the veterans.

When I came to Washington, seeing groups of interns come and go completely reminded me of my experience with FNGs on Guam. The term FNG actually originated out of the Vietnam War, stemming from the U.S. rotation policy with soldiers. When new recruits arrived as FNGs, more veteran soldiers already part way through their tour would have to show them the ropes.

Remember, as a new intern, you are a FNG.

This is part of the reason for the GLARE, and it's also part of the explanation behind the slow friendship phenomenon. Understand that staffers have likely invested a full semester training your intern predecessor, and now you've arrived all bright eyed and bushy tailed, but clueless so now they have to train you. *Staff are glad you've arrived and need your help, but they also dread the learning curve.*

Another aspect of the FNG phenomenon is that, as a new person, you haven't really "earned your spurs" yet, so to speak. Resident office workers may have worked in the trenches together for years. Until you've spent some time there too, you will be regarded as an outsider.

If your new office is one where internship terms overlap such that some interns have been there longer than others, you may find that veteran interns tend to treat the new ones like FNGs. Does this sound a lot like rushing a fraternity or sorority? It is.

You may not be into the Greek thing, but as a new intern, don't be surprised if you have to play that game just a little bit. Remember, your purpose is professional. *You're interning to get access, you're interning to learn.*

Lock and load comrade; being an FNG is part of the path.

66 So a prudent man
should always
follow in the
footsteps of great
men and imitate
those who have
been outstanding. 99

NICCOLO MACHIAVELLI

STEP 13

Tune In

In school, it's logical to expect that you will follow a regular schedule. Certain classes meet at certain times; lunch happens at a certain time; you go home at a certain time. Schools even have bells that go off to signal a change from one time to another.

In the U.S. Senate they have little bells that go off to alert Senators whenever a vote is being called, and of course on Wall Street they open and close with a bell. But that's about as close as most workplaces get to having bells. *In most offices, the signal to switch modes is much more subtle and in my experience, new interns miss it all the time.*

If you walk into an office and things are dead quiet, with people working heads down at their desk – you should adopt the same posture. You might walk into your office and find people shouting and running around urgently. This is not the time to try and ask questions that can wait or engage in idle chitchat. On the other hand, people are kicking back, laughing – talking about stuff that isn't really work related – you can relax to. *The point is: read the signs.*

All Ahead Flank Speed

Have you seen the movie "The Hunt for Red October"? In the film there is a scene where rogue Soviet Submarine Captain Ramius (played by Sean Connery) suddenly asks his crew to increase speed as they're going through a particularly tricky spot near the ocean floor. The crew has to re-plot their course on the fly to avoid smashing into an underwater mountain. Captain Ramius is making his crew sweat on purpose.

You may encounter supervisors during your internship that intentionally chose the most inopportune times to request that you do the most mundane things. They will ask in a way and during a time that makes it almost seem like they are testing you. It will feel that way, because,they are.

So, be ready for this. When you're in the heat of some hectic crisis, be prepared for a supervisor to come up with something extra at the worst time. If and when they do, don't bat an eyelid. Take the request in stride. If you show constant cool under pressure, that will make you stand out as a superduper intern.

So many times when I've been in a situation that was pretty much verging on crisis – people running around, phones going crazy, smoke coming out of peoples' ears – an intern has chosen that opportune time to ask about something that could wait or, even worse, tried to start up some small talk. I think what happens sometimes is that interns know something is going on and they either 1) want to help, or 2) want to be involved, but they're not sure how to do either because they don't really understand what is happening. So, they default to small talk. *Don't be one of these interns.*

If you walk into a situation that is clearly a crisis, and you're not exactly sure what is going on' or how you can help, the best thing to do is stay out of the way. Is it okay to stand to the side so you are available to help if called on? Absolutely. That is actually a good idea. However, be careful not to be a distraction. An intern in this situation should follow Hippocrates' sage advice: "Do no harm."

Whether they know it or not, people tend to like and trust others who look and act like themselves. So, if your intern supervisor is focused like a laser, you should be too. If your supervisor is relaxed, you should be too. Being a mimic will give you increased access and opportunities to learn.

" I carry a badge. "

JOE FRIDAY

Show Your ID

When you start your internship, chances are you're going to be issued some kind of ID badge. In fact, going off to get your ID badge may be one of the first things you're asked to do as an intern. Don't be surprised if you spend at least part of the first day of your internship going to some hard-to-find office where you wind up waiting to get a picture taken (think student ID office).

Some badges are fancier than others. At the low end, you may receive something that looks like it's not much more than a business card. You might look at it once, put it in a drawer, and never think about it again. More than likely though, your badge will have a few more bells and whistles than that. In our increasingly security conscious world, badges are becoming a bigger deal.

Generally, badges consist of some kind of laminated credential that includes your photo, an expiration date, and sometimes your title/office. At the high end, a badge displays your security clearance and contains some kind of magnetic device required to access your workplace.

In very secure workplaces I've seen situations where one is required to show a badge to an officer, then scan the badge, then enter a pin number, then walk through a metal detector. Then, you need the same badge to use the elevator, and eventually get through your office door. These are the sorts of places where badges must be displayed at all times.

Depending on your particular workplace, people may take the security badge stuff very seriously, or not seriously at all. Whatever the case, somewhere at your workplace, somebody has probably written down what the policy is regarding badges. Chances are that whoever that person is, they believe it is their life's purpose to enforce the policy. *Beware: interns are easy prey.*

So, the thing to do is 1) know policy regarding security badges, and be ready to comply with it if somebody gives you grief, but 2) behave the way established staffers behave when it comes to badges.

Why not follow the badge policy to the letter? Well, this may sound crazy, but if you are too much of an eager beaver when it comes to wearing your badge - you can get judged for it. As in, "look at the new intern so proud of their shiny new badge - they are so young..."

Is there anything wrong with being proud of your ID badge? Nope. Let me confess, I've got a drawer full of old ID badges from over the years. They are trophies of experience. However, flaunting a work ID is an intern "tell". You don't want people to be distracted by how you're wearing your badge; you want people to respect you, and focus on how awesome you are.

Believe it or not, during the summertime in Washington, DC interns can sometimes be seen flaunting their intern badges out in public like a status symbol. I've seen young men and women wearing their badges in the grocery store...on a Saturday (and no, it didn't look like they had been working overtime, they just liked their badge).

I've even seen interns try to use their ID badges to try to get into bars and restaurants. This is wrong on so many levels: first, it won't work, because the bouncer doesn't care that you work for Congressman Flung-a-dung. Second, anytime you produce a work ID, it implies you are representing your employer. Last, but not least, if word got back to your employer that you were using a work ID to ask for special privileges in public, they would definitely think you were a dork, would likely be really pissed, and might fire you - not to mention the fact that using a public position for private gain like that is also very illegal.

People wear badges in different ways. Sometimes badges come with little clips or pins that can be attached to a pocket or lapel. Workplace culture permitting, a cooler way to wear a badge is on a lanyard around your neck. You can buy lanyards like this online - they're often made from metal chains or cloth straps. Whatever they are made from, make sure the lanyard you have isn't going to break and cause you to lose your badge.

If you wear an ID around the neck, make sure it rests around the outside of your collar, otherwise it looks weird coming up around the sides of your neck. Also, when you're not at work - take off your badge or at least slip it into a shirt pocket while still around your neck.

A work ID may seem new to you, but consider that staffers may have had one of these things around their neck for 15 or 30 years. Don't be surprised if you see colleagues on staff twirling their badge or playing with it. *Make no mistake, in the workplace, an ID badge can affect a person's identity in more ways than one.* Even if only subconsciously, your colleagues are going to be hyper-aware of how you wear and otherwise handle your ID badge. Treat it like something you've been wearing for 30 years, and people might even give you the same respect they would someone who has worn an ID for that long.

" They had to
replace my metal
plate in my head
with a plastic one. **"**

COUSIN EDDIE

Shield Your Magnetic Personality

I n the summer, Washington, DC can get hot. Not just regular hot, but swampy Degobah, Yoda-like hot. I grew up in the tropics and I understand humidity. But the thing about the tropics is, most folks don't make you wear a suit in the tropics. If you're working in a muggy American U.S. city – work clothes can be a bit of drag.

There is almost nothing worse than walking around outside, in your work clothes in DC in the summer, except when you reach the entrance to your air conditioned destination only to find the entry way blocked by an intern fishing for loose coins, trying to get through a metal detector.

Damn.

Want to engender good will amongst your colleagues? *Don't be the new intern who holds things up at the metal detector.*

This might sound like a simple thing, but getting through the metal detector actually takes a little forethought. If the entrance to your workplace is guarded by a metal detector, make sure you can produce (and then later retrieve) all magnetic contraband (phones, blackberry, and coins) for the x-ray machine in one motion.

Remember, at the same time you do this, you'll also likely need to display your ID badge too.

On the first day of your internship, decide where you're going to make a habit of keeping all your metallic stuff…before long, going through the metal detector will become automatic. Ladies, keep the shiny jewelry in your bag till you've passed through the magnetometers; and dudes, forget about wearing any kind of shoes with steel in them.

Remember, during the day you may be called on to enter/exit the building on short notice. If your supervisor says "come with me" and winds up taking you through a metal detector, don't be the intern that requires your boss to slow down while you get your act together. More than likely your supervisor will assume that, like interns she's worked with in the past, you will require extra time to go through the metal detector. *Surprise her.*

“ Not all who
wander are lost. ”

J.R.R. TOLKIEN

Find A Place To Dwell

When you find out that you've been accepted into an internship program, it seems logical to assume that during your internship – somebody will point to a desk and say, "Welcome! This is your desk!"

It seems like you would be right to expect something like that. Except that, if I agreed with you, we'd both be wrong.

You might have the fortunate situation where your office assigns you a desk that is meant for just you for the duration of your internship. But, more than likely – you will be lucky to have any place to work (desk, chair, computer, and phone) on any given day, much less a permanent set-up devoted just to you.

In today's cost cutting, mobile, start-up world, it's not unusual to see permanent staffers fighting it out for workspace. As an intern who is even lower on the totem pole, available workspace for you may sometimes be slim pickings.

Who Wore It Best?

Pretend you are a big huge gigantic boss walking around an office - the sort that can decide to hire, or not hire, new interns as staff.

You see two interns: the first one is just kind of standing there, or maybe talking to somebody else. When you ask them what they are doing, the intern replies, "I'm waiting for a desk because I don't have a place to work."

The second intern you see is sitting on the floor working on something furiously. When you ask what they are doing the intern says, "I'm working on this important project because it needs to get done."

Which intern do you think the big boss is going to have more sympathy, admiration and gratitude for? Which intern will that boss remember when it comes time to hire?

So what should you do? How can you do your work if you don't have a place to work? Well my friend, if you're going to be a stellar intern, it's time to get creative. First of all, you've got to be bold. *That means if there is physically an empty space available to do your work, assume it's up for grabs unless somebody tells you otherwise.* Don't ask for permission, ask for forgiveness.

Obviously, the less senior person's space you can hijack, the better. When faced with a shortage of workspace, most interns will do a 180 degree turn back to their supervisor and say, "I need a place to work." Instead of solving the problem on their own, the intern hands their problem over to their supervisor.

Be different. Look for desks that aren't being used because somebody is out sick, or at a long meeting, or on vacation or whatever. Do everything you can to avoid messing up their space by one iota, and be ready to vacate the space at a moment's notice, but don't stand around with work to do because you're afraid to use an empty workspace.

If this philosophy makes you uncomfortable, think of it this way. The workplace where you are interning has invested tons of resources to establish an office and, presumably, the work you have been tasked to do is important. *An unused desk and an idle intern are wasted resources.* Be bold, sit down and do your work. If somebody more senior shows up, vacate immediately. In the meantime, do your thing.

When you can't find a place to work in the office (or if staffers have kicked you out), think about what you might be able to do without a desk, or by sharing a desk. If part of your work involves just phone calls, find a phone (a courtesy phone, a cell phone, etc.), and make your calls. If you need web access, bring your laptop from home (if you've got one), and march yourself down to the nearest coffee shop that has free Wi-Fi. Sometimes organizations have rules about working off site or with using personal equipment. But unless somebody tells you not to do it, do it – and for God's sake, don't ask permission. Chances are, if you don't raise the question, no one else will. This is especially true if the work you are doing is important and you are finding a way to get it done, overcoming any barriers you encounter on your own.

When Hillary Clinton was sworn into the U.S. Senate in January of 2001, I helped move her office from the White House to a very small, cramped transition office in the basement of the Dirksen Senate Building. As Senator Clinton's office quickly accumulated new staff in order to serve the constituents of New York, we had to get creative in terms of office space.

By March of that year we literally had built a peninsula of desks pushed end to end. In order to get to their desks, some staffers had to traverse an area we called the Cape of Good Hope – all the way past everyone else's desk – to get to their desk. At that time, we were especially slammed with people wanting to meet with the new Senator's office. So, we took meetings in the cafeteria down the hall, or if need be, literally standing in the hallway. Until we received access to our permanent office, the interns we hosted that first spring literally didn't have a place to sit, ever. They were busy and did all their work on foot, usually standing outside in the hall.

If you find yourself in a situation like that with your internship and it bothers you, consider this: I could be wrong, but my sense is that the best internships are often ones that place an intern in a little bit of chaos like this. Why? Because if an organization is really vital and active and flying close to the edge in terms of what they do, chances are they won't be stable enough to field enough desks for everybody. *When you are interning for an organization that is truly growing and making a difference in the world, sometimes there are more important things than having a desk, much less one of your own.*

"Concentrate all your thoughts upon the work at hand. The sun's rays do not burn until brought to a focus.**"**

ALEXANDER GRAHAM BELL

Show Up And Be Present

Show up and be present. This advice can be found on lots of "Tips for Success" lists, but it has special meaning for those wishing to achieve intern awesomeness.

It might not feel like it sometimes, but as an intern, one advantage you may have over more veteran staffers is that you are fresh. Sure, older, more established workers might have access to greater resources, but they also likely have a lot more responsibilities, baggage, and frankly, are much more singed with signs of burn-out. You, on the other hand, can be much more present.

For example, established staffers in the office may be dealing with mortgages, lawns to mow, kids, aging parents, etc. If you're like most interns, your biggest worry may be, "Where should I order pizza from tonight?" Don't get me wrong, I love pizza too. My point here is that you have the ability to be present a lot more at work than most people, and you can use this to your advantage. Yes, I know you have schoolwork to do, but trust me – you've still got less demands on your time than most of the people you work with.

Chances are, compared to the veterans in your office, you are younger, have more energy, are in better shape, have fewer personal obligations and have much greater flexibility in your schedule than others in your office. *Use this to your advantage.*

Not too long after my internship at the White House (when I had been hired as a permanent staffer), King Hassan II of Morocco died. The news came late in the afternoon. Within a few hours, the decision was made that President Clinton and the First Lady, along with several former Presidents and a bunch really important people, would attend the funeral. Following Islamic tradition, the funeral was going to happen fast. This meant that the Presidential Advance Team would need to leave immediately.

Following my usual practice of staying later than most, that evening I was summarily recruited from my desk to be the Deputy Lead of that Advance Team. Within hours, I was on a C-130 bound for Rabat and one of the best adventures I've ever had. I could go on a trip like that with almost no notice because I was young, had no real obligations, and was crazy enough to do it. As an intern, you should be too. *During your internship be present, and be ready to take advantage of opportunities.*

Be the first one at the office, and the last one to leave. It sounds twisted, but there is nothing more impressive to an intern supervisor than arriving at work and seeing an intern standing in the hallway because that intern got there so early that they arrived before the doors were unlocked. Obviously this isn't a trick you need to do every day – but it's an excellent way to show your dedication, and for you to stand out from the crowd.

Be one of the last if not the last person to leave the office. If your supervisors are ordering you to leave, then leave. But otherwise, hang around. In my experience, the biggest crises (aka opportunities) often break after hours when there are just a few people around. If you are one of those few people, you're going to be able to offer tons of value to the staffers who are there. You might even save the day without realizing it.

When you leave your office, there is no need to talk about office stuff outside the office. Now, don't get me wrong, if your parents or your faculty advisor ask you about your internship, tell them about it. But, there is no need to blabber on about work in public places (busses, parks, Facebook, etc.).

I was once in line at a store behind two young women who, wearing their work IDs out for all to see, I quickly identified as interns from a particular organization. I couldn't help but overhear their conversation. They were going on and on about this event they were helping to put together, and how their organization was going to list Senator Clinton as a confirmed speaker on the invitation, regardless of whether she could come or not, just so they would get a good turnout. They had no idea that Hillary Clinton's scheduler was standing right behind them. Let me assure you – that organization got an earful from me the next day. *Remember, when it comes to work stuff, you never know who is listening.*

The same thing goes with paper. *If you've got documents or records or flash drives you're working on at work, leave them at work* – unless there is a real reason you need to have them outside of work. The rationale is that if you aren't carrying stuff around, you can't lose it. Shortly before I started interning at the White House, an intern got in huge trouble because they decided it would be cool to take home a copy of the President's schedule to show their friends. Unfortunately, on their way home, they managed to leave the schedule on a park bench seat. Somebody else found it and turned it in to the Secret Service.

When you are at work, be present at work. Beyond getting there early and staying late, make sure that you're around. If other interns are going for long lunches, be the one intern who stays behind and is always THERE. Time bathroom breaks so they happen when you're least likely be needed. Bring lunch from home so you won't have to spend time going to get lunch (we'll talk more about this later). This may sound extreme, but trust me – it's worth it. By being around as much as you can, especially while others are away someplace else, you greatly increase your chances of standing out above the crowd.

I'll talk about this more later, but during your internship make sure you get into the habit of having your cell phone always charged and close by, so you are reachable. More than that, make sure your supervisors and especially the people who are doing the cool work you'd like to be more involved in know how to reach you if they ever need to reach you. *Make sure everybody knows that you are available to help them if they need it.*

About a month into my White House internship one of the big bosses on the First Lady's staff asking me out of the blue, "Eric, what time will you get here tomorrow?" My immediate response was "Whatever time you tell me!" It turned out that they wanted me to be there the next morning at 4 am to help prepare for an early morning interview the First Lady was doing for the Today Show. I was there at 3:45 am, and it was one of the coolest things I got to do during my internship. If I hadn't been right there when they were looking for somebody to help, or if I'd balked at the idea of such an early morning, I would have missed out big time.

Some interns are hard workers, but they forget to be present because they are so focused on the future. For example, I've seen interns who were great for a couple of weeks, but then they clearly started to become distracted with thoughts about the future. Instead of laser-like focus on "this is what I need to do now", they started to worry about "how long will I need to intern here before they hire me?" This is a common mistake. During your internship BE PRESENT and the rest will follow. As Yoda admonishes Luke in the *Empire Strikes Back*, "Ready are you? What know, ready? For 800 years have I trained Jedi. My own counsel will I keep on who is to be trained! A Jedi must have the deepest commitment. Hmm? The most serious mind! This one a long time have I watched. All his life has he looked away, to the future. To the horizon. Never his mind on where he was! Hmm? What he was doing! Huh. Adventure. Eh! Excitement. Eh! A Jedi craves not these things. You are reckless!"

When you first start your internship, your supervisor will likely ask you to commit to a particular schedule. If they don't ask you to do this, then you should commit a certain schedule to yourself, and then share what that schedule will be with your supervisor. Either way, once you make that commitment, stick to it.

This means no "I'm sorry I was late" or "I would have been here on time, but there was so much traffic…" Stick to your commitment. If you do, it will create an incredible contrast between you and many of your intern colleagues.

Now, if something comes up (an exam, an important paper, a cool opportunity, whatever), you ASK your supervisor whether you can do something different from the schedule you have committed to. That's fine. What most interns do is TELL their supervisor that they are making a change, or worse, they just do it without asking or telling anybody.

Here's another tip about being present that even a lot of seasoned staffers get wrong. If you get this right as an intern, you'll go far. *Either be at work, or don't – but don't try and be in between.* If you are feeling bad and decide you are too sick to work, then call in sick, and let that be that. Don't call in sick and then still try and work a little bit from your deathbed. If you are too sick to work, then you are obliged to give up your responsibilities to somebody who is well. Let go, get better, then come back when you are well.

This idea is more important than some people realize. When workers are sick, they will often do one of two things. Sometimes, people will come into the office even though they are sick and risk making everybody else sick – but then they do kind of a half ass job of working because, after all, they are sick! Other times, people will call in sick, but then dictate that nobody can do their work but them – so the whole operation becomes bottle-necked by one person.

If you come into the office to do your internship, be present and be at 100%. If you are indeed not feeling well, then go home and get better. Be present or go away; you can't do both at the same time.

66 You can always
amend a big plan,
but you can never
expand a little
one. I don't
believe in little
plans. I believe in
plans big enough
to meet a
situation which we
can't possibly
foresee now. 99

HARRY S. TRUMAN

Prevent, Predict, Problem Solve

When I was training to be a scuba instructor, one of things I learned was the importance of preventing situations where problems might occur, predicting when problems might occur, and managing problems when they did occur.

During my internship, I never ceased to be amazed by how often I used this same philosophy in the office. Likewise, of the hundreds of interns I've supervised over the years – the best interns are always able to prevent, predict and problem solve. During your internship, you should focus on this too.

One skill that is often not taught in school, but that I've found useful in the workplace both as a staffer and an intern, is the art of contingency planning. It is second nature to me now, but I remember when I was fresh out of school – I never put as much emphasis on contingency planning as I do now.

What do I mean by contingency planning? *Contingency planning is the habit of always having plan B, plan C, and even a plan D up your sleeve for pretty much everything you do.* For example, let's say somebody asks you to make 5 copies of a single paged document. How many contingencies can you come up with?

In that situation, this is the sequence that would happen in my mind right off the bat: Photocopy, 5 copies. What if I forget the instruction? How could I handle that? Where is the nearest copier? Where are the two nearest after that? What if the first copier is out of paper? Where is the paper? What if it has a paper jam from the last person who used it? How easy is that copier to clear? What if that copier is out of toner? Where is the extra toner? Do I know how to change the toner? If I'm not sure about one of these questions, who might know the answers? If they're not around, who else might know? How can I reach them? If all else fails, what is my holy s#$@ plan?

Chances are, you or I would walk up to that first copier, hit a button, and everything would be fine. But – if the universe throws a curve ball at you – you'll be way better off if you've spent even a moment thinking about contingencies.

How was Scotty always able to give Kirk Warp 6 when, just a little earlier, the Engineer swore to the Captain that the Enterprise could only go Warp 5? Scotty was an excellent contingency planner, and he made a habit of always holding a little extra in reserve.

How can you become a great contingency planner during your internship? A good first step is to learn the landscape of your workplace.

Snoop around. Look in cabinets, notice where the First Aid kit is, notice who has what kind of cell phone charger, pay attention.

Run exercises in your mind. Make a habit of asking yourself things like, "How would I help my boss if a pen exploded in his shirt pocket?"

Walk A Mile In Your Boss' Shoes

Everybody has particular preferences and when it comes right down to it, nobody can predict what another person will like or dislike all the time. However, if you get into the habit of giving just a little bit of extra thought about how you can add value to your internship organization, it can make a huge difference.

For example, suppose you are preparing a binder full of documents for a supervisor. Before you hand off your work, stop, take a breath, and pretend for a moment that you are your boss in the exact situation your boss will be when they need that binder. Is there any way your work could be better? Are the tabs arranged in a useful, legible way? Are the materials in the binder organized in a way that is the most useful? Is the binder labeled in such a way that it isn't likely to be mistaken for another? Is there too much info in the binder? Is there not enough?

Nobody's work is ever perfect. Work product can always be better. However, a habit that will set you apart from other interns is the practice of always thinking about how your work might be improved, and then doing one or two little things to make it better every time. When you do work in an office, especially when you're under the magnifying glass of an internship, try and improve your work just a little bit every day – then repeat.

Ask things like, "how bad would it be if the hard drive with that important project failed? What could I do to mitigate against a disaster like that?"

The idea is not to become obsessed with every possible calamity, but rather, as the Scouts say, to "Be Prepared." *If you've done just a little thinking about how you would handle big disasters, then you'll be more than ready to handle every day challenges.* That is the mark of great intern.

Here is another benefit to contingency planning: you will get to the point where you can anticipate tasks before people ask you to do them. There is almost nothing more satisfying than when a boss, especially a demanding boss, asks you to do something - or even complains about why you haven't done something - and you can reply, "Already did it."

Most interns don't take the time to study their workplace or the people in it. If you do, even just a little, you can be a psychic intern. Let me tell you, nobody messes with a psychic intern. *Psychic interns get respect.*

66 I have eight
different bosses
right now. 99

PETER GIBBONS

Manage Your Manager

The whole concept of the classroom is pretty much built around the idea "follow the teacher's instructions, do what the teacher says." Most students who take on internships make the natural leap in logic that when they enter the work place, their boss assumes a role similar to that of a teacher.

Sorry, that answer is incorrect. That's a chip up the nose, I'm afraid.

In the workplace, management and leadership is often more of a two-way street. That is, as much as bosses manage their subordinates… sometimes it's the other way around. During your internship, you should be prepared to take a step forward. *When the situation calls for it, be ready to take initiative and manage your supervisor.* This sometimes takes some subtle maneuvering and savvy, but if you're able to master this skill – you'll go far.

I once heard a story about a well-known political operative. This particular person is incredibly smart and influential, but also has a legendary temper who some find difficult to work under. Three weeks into a particular campaign, he had gone through three interns - nobody was making him happy. In a fourth attempt, the campaign intern coordinator paired him up with April. On April's first day - before she'd really even met her new boss – he was inside his office ranting and raving, "God damn those sons-of-bitches! Damn it!" Then he called out "Get those sons-of bitches on the phone right now!"

Having no idea what or who the boss was talking about, April called back "Which sons-of-bitches would you like me to get on the phone, sir?" She was a success in that job for the rest of the campaign.

It's not always true, but in my experience, in the workplace there is often a direct correlation between seniority and a boss' need to be managed from below. In the office, everybody can use some help sometimes with getting organized, setting boundaries and talking through ideas. The big bosses are lonely up there on top; they can use management from below. *Interns are often in a great position to do this, because they don't pose any threat of upsetting office politics.*

If you are assigned to a big boss during your internship, don't be a shrinking violet. Step forward. Chances are, the bigger the boss, the more help they'll need. If you see a messy desk – get in there and help them get organized. Take care not to mess up their business, but push the envelope little by little. If you cross a boundary (i.e. where did that piece of paper go?!?), you'll know soon enough. Most likely however, they'll be pleasantly surprised by your initiative and will encourage it. *Help your boss solve problems they don't even know they have.*

Pay attention. If your supervisor likes a certain drink, help them find a way to have that on hand always. If they like to write with a certain pen, make sure you have a supply. Look for things that need to get done that have been sitting around for months – take initiative there. If the boss hasn't been able to take action on something that has been sitting around for that long, chances are they aren't going to mind if you take a stab at it. *Don't overstep your limits right out of the gate, take baby steps.*

We'll get into this a bit later, but often interns run into situations where they have nothing to do because they don't spend any time looking for things they can do. If you wait for your boss to give you every assignment, you'll most likely be bored. Instead, look for assignments you can give yourself. If your boss isn't being a good supervisor , start assigning tasks to yourself. I promise this will get their attention.

> "The great defense against the air menace is to attack the enemy's aircraft as near as possible to their point of departure."

WINSTON CHURCHILL

Slay Dragons

The notion of managing your manager pre-supposes, of course, that your boss is a relatively decent human being; that as a mentor, they have an interest in your education and that they want to see you succeed.

Some bosses are hard, but it doesn't necessarily mean they are bad. In fact, some of the best bosses I've had have been incredibly demanding with unbelievably high expectations. Like a tough coach, a tough boss can be great because they are able to get you to do things you never thought you could do.

However, there is a big difference between bosses like this, and Dragons.

Dragons are bosses in the workplace who, for whatever reason, are just mean. The hallmark of a dragon is disrespect. A boss can be tough, even yell about things. But, if their concerns remain focused on the work and they remain respectful of you as a person – that's legit.

On the other hand, if you are faced with a supervisor who is just a bully, someone who directs their criticism towards your worth as a human being, then you've got to slay them – fast. The very moment you're sure they've crossed the line – you've got to respond. How do you know you're sure? As a great intern you've thought it through, because you do contingency planning, right?

If you're having a difficult time with your boss, do some thinking about where your red line lies. Do the mental exercise where you determine what kind of criticism is acceptable, and what is not.

Prepared in this way, you won't have to think about whether your supervisor has crossed the line during the heat of battle, you'll just know. If/when a supervisor does cross that line, you've got to push back right away. I once had a boss who pretty much told me I didn't listen and was stupid – she wasn't referring to my work...she was criticizing my value as a person. So, I let her have it. I shed any air of subordination and explained in no uncertain terms that I required her never to speak like that to me ever again, because it negatively affected the work I was trying to accomplish for her. Did she fire me? Nope. Did she yell back at me? Nope. She backed the hell off. That's what bullies do when you push back.

When someone who is your supervisor acts or speaks to you in *appropriately, they step out of their role as your boss.* When this happens, you can likewise step out of your role as their subordinate with a professionally clean conscious.

On another occasion, I had a boss who was just badgering me verbally about the tasks she had wanted me to do, repeatedly asking me the same questions over and over not to get the answer, or to make sure I understood the assignment or to motivate me. Her goal was clearly just to harass me – I was sure. So, I slew the Dragon. I changed modes and asked her "have you forgotten my response when I answered these same questions just a few moments ago? Do you remember the conversation we just had about this? I feel like you are asking these questions just to badger me. Is that true? If so, then why?" She didn't expect that, and she stopped.

In truth, bosses may be bad managers or incompetent, but you will rarely find one that is openly disrespectful to subordinates. In my career, I've only run into two or three. However, if you run into a boss who disrespectful (verbally,

Remember, You're Not Their First

If you're dealing with an internship supervisor who is a true bully, chances are you're not their first victim. In fact, most likely the issue of that supervisor's ability to manage subordinates has come up before with that supervisor's supervisor. Bullies in the workplace are usually sensitive to people accusing them of being a bully because they have a history of being a bully.

As an intern faced with a bully supervisor you may feel that your word won't count for anything against a supervisor. But remember, chances are you're not the first person to cry wolf. If you're right about your supervisor being a bully, there is likely a thick personnel file someplace with similar complaints. Bullies don't want that file to get any thicker.

physically, whatever) don't be shy about explicitly telling them to stop. *If they don't stop, get help from somebody else.*

In the workplace, you should expect people to be tough as nails about the work, but if they are ever disrespectful to you as a person, don't tolerate it for a second. Slay any dragons you meet right away, and don't look back.

66 We herd sheep, we drive cattle, we lead people. Led me, follow me, or get out of my way. **99**

GEORGE PATTON

Shun and Lead the Herd

On your first day of elementary school, high school, or college – you might not have realized it at the time – the people you happened to make friends with first likely had a huge impact on your social life for years to come. When you are in a situation where everybody is new, your best friend may become the person you just happen to sit next to at lunch, etc. The same is often true on the first day of an internship.

On the first day of an internship, like the first day of school, it's a little nerve wracking. Everybody is in a new place with new people, the urge to find some sort of group, to find a place to belong quickly, can be overwhelming.

But remember – there is a reason you've worked so hard to land this internship. Your first priority is not to make friends. I know this sounds harsh – but you can find friends lots of other places. *Your internship is the place to focus on learning new skills, and getting access to people who can help with your professional goals.*

So on that first day of your internship you may see lots of other interns acting like it's the first day of school, banding together, relating with each other. There will be gossip, people hooking up - all the normal stuff. That's fine, but I don't want you to follow that herd. Take the path less traveled. Be the intern who stands out because they are focused more on work, less on the social scene. By doing this you will come across to everybody, both staff and other interns, as way more mature – and everybody will respect you more for it.

Don't get me wrong, you don't have to be a snob or a cold fish – just be the intern who is focused like a laser. In fact, with this strategy you can quickly become a leader among other interns.

During your internship put yourself in the position where other interns are coming to you for help. Whenever they do – go out of your way to help them. People on staff will notice this more than you know. After all, a great way to show that you're ready to graduate from intern to staffer - that you're ready to be hired - is to be the intern that winds up supervising and helping other interns naturally.

Sometimes interns wind up being incredibly competitive with other interns – you want to avoid this path. Dwight Eisenhower once said, "you can get a lot done if you don't worry about who gets the credit." Go out of your way to make others in your office, both other interns and staffers, look good. If a boss praises you for work that someone else had a part in, make sure you receive the praise by recognizing whoever else deserves credit.

Even if you are a brand new intern, come in with the mindset that your job is to help staffers and other interns. *Constantly look for opportunities to do this.*

" You're going to
like the way
you look. **"**

George Zimmer
(Men's Warehouse dude)

The Last Suit You'll Ever Wear

Adolescence can be kind of tricky – all these weird things happen to your body. It takes a while to learn how to deal with all those physical changes. Believe it or not – and this is something most interns never understand going into their first internship – maintaining yourself as a professional takes some adjustment too!

If you're interning in a place that requires daily professional dress, you've got to develop some habits you may never have needed before. First off, you've got to have the right clothes; they don't necessarily need to be super expensive, but you've got to have the right duds. If you're not sure what the right clothes are, do a little research. Find some professional pictures of the most important men and women who work at the organization where you will be interning – you need to dress as much like them as possible.

Most professional clothes require maintenance, and a little planning. Before your internship starts, figure out what dry cleaner you are going to use and how often you need to get to them. Make sure the dry cleaner's hours and turn-around time are going to work for you, especially if you only have a few sets of work clothes. You'll need a plan for keeping your shoes shined and in good shape. Make sure you have easy, regular access to an iron and an ironing board. Learn how to use it. Dudes, do you know how to tie a tie?

One time there was an intern walking around the halls of the White House – this guy was wearing a shirt that was crazy wrinkled along with a tie that had a bunch of golf clubs on it. A senior staffer approached this intern and said, "Young man! Do you own an iron?"

This poor kid was so clueless, he thought she was talking about a golf iron, so he replied, "Yes! I own a full set of clubs." Yeah... that guy got sent home that day. Get an iron.

If you have never had to wear office clothing every day, it takes a while to get used to and is way easier to mess up during the day than the sturdier threads you a probably used to wearing. If you have a place to stash it, keep some extra stuff at work, just in case you forget your socks or tie, or pants, etc.

During my first internship I had the good fortune of living just a few blocks from the White House. Knowing this, an intern colleague of mine once begged me to let him go borrow an extra shirt from my place. He had gotten sunburned at the beach that weekend, and he now had blisters popping all over his back and through his dress shirt – really, really nasty. At the time, I only owned three shirts – just enough to have a clean one every day. So, I told that guy he was on his own (yeah, it was really gross – poor bastard).

Ladies, this is outside my area, but be smart out how much skin you show. Don't hold back, be a fashionista, glam it up! But be a distraction because of how awesome your work is, not because of how low your neckline goes.

Shoes are another area where I've seen interns have trouble. New interns tend to run a lot of errands, may not have an actual chair to sit down in – they tend to be on their feet a lot. If your feet aren't used to wearing dress shoes or you're trying to get by in shoes that don't fit really well – you're toast.

A trick I learned from Secret Service agents (they get to stand all day long) is to get shoes that are a little loose – feet tend to swell through the day. Ladies, if you're going to wear heels, make sure they are the type you can do battle in. If you need to, wear sneakers to and from work – change when you arrive. Gents, I don't know about you, but I look for the thickest soles I can find. Old government buildings tend to have granite floors that like to eat shoes.

> **Humanity's fate has been sealed. You will be destroyed.**

Q

Everybody is Human

The Matrix, Terminator, Battlestar Galactica…how many movies have you seen where machines decide they need to rid the world of humanity because people are just too damn messy?

Believe it or not (red pill or blue pill), but you should expect that your internship will be a little bit like the Matrix. Yes, you will have super powers. Yes, you can create your own reality. But more importantly for our discussion here – you are the messy human, surrounded by machines, being judged.

In today's office world we are all increasingly surrounded by and dependent on technology. As a result, for better or worse (probably for worse), most people in the office are expected to perform with machine -like efficiency and sterility. It may not be right, but in the office world – especially as an intern - keep your biological impact to a minimum.

This means: don't be the intern with horrible breath. Don't be the sweaty intern or the intern that smells terrible. Get it?

I once had an intern who had a habit of sneezing incredibly loud – such that every time he sneezed (and he sneezed a lot), it brought the office to a standstill. If it was a medical problem, people might have understood – but this wasn't the case with this intern. Rather, this kid just liked to sneeze really loud – he didn't make any effort to tone it down. This intern could have been the greatest worker in the world and it wouldn't have mattered. The only thing people associated with this intern was that he sneezed really loudly. Don't be like this.

Make extra effort to do the simple things – preferably in a private place - before you appear in the office. Blow your nose, brush your teeth, pop a mint, brush your hair – whatever you have to do in order to get yourself together. My wife once worked with a person who had a habit of combing his beard during office meetings. Intern: do not do this!

People in close office quarters have all sorts of pet peeves. As the intern, people are going to tolerate your biological leavings less than anybody. So, don't chew gum. If you're going to sneeze, cough, hiccup, burp or God knows what else…step outside the office, if you can.

In the movie *The Shawshank Redemption*, Morgan Freeman plays a man recently paroled from jail who has found work at a grocery store. Having been under lock and key for so long, Freeman's character keeps asking the grocery store manager if it is alright to go to the bathroom. The manager corrects him, "you don't have to ask every time to go to the bathroom, just go, ok?"

You are a grown up. Not only that, but an office is not the same as jail. So, as an intern, don't feel like you have to ask every time you need to excuse yourself. If you act like a grown up, people will give you the benefit of the doubt that when you excuse yourself, there must be a good reason.

If you are thoughtful about your personal space and the effect your presence has on the office environment, you will be showing wisdom beyond most interns' years. This means, keep your cell phone on buzz and don't leave it behind when you leave your seat. Avoid bringing smelly food into the office for lunch. If you play sound from your computer, keep it really low or use head phones.

You may find that others in the office, especially more senior staffers, aren't so considerate. As an intern wanting to get ahead, your

Sleep It Off

This is something you actually SHOULD have learned in school, but just in case you didn't…

If you want to be sharp during your internship, you've got to get some sleep. It also helps to do the other stuff (eat right, drink water, exercise), but if you just get enough sleep, you'll do well.

I've actually had interns that drew my attention at work during the middle of the day because they were snoring. I have no problem with somebody catching a nap during a break at work, but these snoring interns weren't really on break – they just conked out because they were hung over from partying to all hours the night before. Don't be one of these interns.

If you're thinking, "I don't need somebody to tell me this, I'm not a child" – that's good. Then you already know.

best play in the short term is to tolerate it. Just remember though, when you are the boss, be more considerate.

If more senior people in the office like the office dark, don't turn the lights on. When the high ranking staffer in an office likes the office at 68 degrees, then don't mess with the thermostat. You can always bring a small lamp. You can wear a sweater. If the big kahuna in the office plays annoying music, pop on some head phones. Get it? Go out of your way to avoid polluting the office and find ways to mitigate the effect of supervisors messing up your space. Later in your career when you're working with peers or subordinates, you'll be able to tell them to be quiet, turn on the lights, turn up the thermostat and get rid of their smelly food.

I've seen so many interns, who were awesome workers, completely undermine their track record by not carrying themselves appropriately in the office. The modern day persecution of smoking has no respite in the office world. If you're a smoker, hide it and, if you can – don't let the habit be the reason you're in the office less.

In an office, people have an unconscious respect for colleagues that bring their lunch. Brown bagging it signals that you have your act together enough to plan lunch ahead, and that you are smart enough to save money by bringing lunch to work. So, if you can, bring your lunch to work. While everybody else is off spending money to buy lunch, you'll be ready to catch that opportunity, which everyone else is going to miss.

It's okay to make or take personal calls from the office – just don't do it a lot at the beginning of your internship, and don't make it a regular thing. Do it only when you need to do it. It goes back to the idea that, if you act like a grown-up, that's how people will treat you.

When you're out of the office, maintain the professional habit of keeping your cell phone/blackberry/whatever very charged. *Be the intern that is always reachable, who almost always answers the phone.* This is a habit I learned when cell phones were just coming into vogue during my time as an intern in First Lady Hillary Clinton's Office.

Years later, when I served as her Scheduler on Capitol Hill, Senator Clinton would occasionally call during off hours to inquire about something on her schedule. On one of these occasions, she called and noticed that I was particularly out of breath. When Senator Clinton asked why I was so winded, I explained that at that particular moment I was running mile 18 of a marathon. I'm not sure how many points that particular instance of being so reachable got me with the boss, but she shouted "Go Eric!" and reassured me that I shouldn't worry about her question just then. It was enough of a boost to get me to the finish line, that's for sure.

PART FOUR

You Need Mad Skills

Step #24:
Stand Out In Time

Step #25:
Keep Your Desk Insanely Neat

Step #26:
Become a Filing Ninja

Step #27:
The Mighty Pen

Step #28:
Party Like Your
Career Depends On It

Step #29:
Let's Meet

Step #30:
I Can't Do It!
She's Breakin' Apart!

66 We're putting new coversheets on all the TPS reports before they go out now. So if you could go ahead and try to remember to that from now on, that'd be great. All right! 99

BILL LUMBERGH

Step #31:
Your "Back To Internship" List

Step #32:
Don't Be Bored

"How did it get so
late so soon?"

DR. SEUSS

Stand Out In Time

On any "tips for young professionals" list, being on time is one of the most common items. Being on time is one of the easiest ways to stand out from the crowd, but it's also something that most people fail to do.

Three words: BE ON TIME. *Always – not sometimes – always.*

If you're supposed to get work at 8 am, be there at 8 am…with whatever morning drink you need in hand, with breakfast in your belly. Be ready to go. The typical new intern is on time their first couple of days, but then it quickly goes downhill when they see the example of others in the workplace. In most offices, people aren't on time. When they do arrive – the first part of the day is kind of a warm up. They get coffee, they get breakfast, they surf news on the web.

Do not follow this example. Be the intern who is on time. As I stated earlier, if you can make a good impression by getting to work early…then definitely be there early. If you can manage it, be the intern that arrives before your boss and departs after your boss. *Be the intern who is the first in, the first to have their computer booted up, the first to be ready to go.*

If someone calls a meeting or schedules a conference call for 2:00 pm, show up or call in at 2:00 pm. Chances are, by being on time, you'll be the first to arrive other than the meeting organizer. This means you get one-on-one time with whoever that is. Before the meeting time, think about whom the meeting organizer is and what questions you would like to ask them. That person will greatly appreciate your being on time, and be more than willing to chat for a moment while others are dragging themselves in.

Staffers and even your boss might be late or even completely forget about meetings, but that doesn't mean you should. Stand out in your office by being the only intern – and likely the only person – who is consistently on time.

66 The moral
sense is the first
excellence of well-
organized man. 99

THOMAS JEFFERSON

Keep Your Desk Insanely Neat

This is another part of office life where the vast majority of people fall down on the job. You can tell a tremendous amount about somebody by how they keep their desk.

Over the years I've walked into hundreds of offices – the state of one's desk says as much about someone as just about anything else. Most people maintain piles of paper all over the place – this is not good. *As an intern, if you maintain the habit of keeping your desk extremely neat – people will notice.*

At the beginning of your internship, assuming you actually get your own desk, there is a good chance that it will be messed up. Knowing that they are just going to be there temporarily, prior generations of interns may have neglected to make the investment to clean things up.

One of your first tasks as a new intern, no matter what shape your workspace is in, should be to clean it up and get it organized. It's a good bet that most of things in or on your desk can be gotten rid of. But, if you're worried about getting rid of something important, get yourself an empty photocopier paper box and chuck anything that might be important in there temporarily. If after a month or two into your internship nothing has been needed – kill everything in that box.

Even if the duration of your internship is short, act as if you're going to be at that desk for the next 20 years. Obviously, if you are sharing that desk space with other interns, talk to your intern colleagues about how you can effectively share the space. Whatever your particular case may be, remedying a messy desk situation is really important for two reasons. First, if your desk is messy, you're not going to be able to work in an organized, efficient, clear manner. Second, if you have a messy workspace, others will assume it's your mess, and they'll judge you accordingly.

Consider it from a staffer's point of view. If I'm a staffer with a really important project that I need help with, am I going to choose the intern who has a really messy desk? More likely, I'm going to ask for help from the intern who has a desk that says, "I have my act together and I'm not going to lose anything you give me."

In fact, if you display a knack for being organized and keeping a neat workspace, don't be surprised if others in the office, including big bosses, ask you to help them organize their workspace. If a senior person in your office asks if you would be willing to help them get organized, the correct answer is "yes." More than that – keep an eye out for people in the office you'd like to work with who happen to have a messy desk. Ask if you can help them organize their workspace – you never know…they might really welcome the offer.

The Clutter of Your Mind

You may not realize it, but the state of your surroundings has a huge effect on your ability to be creative and productive as an intern. When you are surrounded by clutter, your mind is also filled with clutter.

As an intern you may not have a lot of control over your office surroundings, but take measures to enhance the aesthetic of your workspace as far as you can. It's a small thing, but it will definitely give you an edge.

66 If you file your
waste paper basket
for fifty years,
you have a
public library. **99**

TONY BENN

Become a Filing Ninja

The big reason so many interns and people in an office have messy workspaces is because they have never learned the correct way to file paper. As a result, random piles of paper accumulate over weeks, months, and years.

With the onset of digital information, the paper problem is lessening somewhat…but there are still plenty of traditional office packrats out there. Here are my rules about filing. Follow these rules, and help others in your office to follow these rules, and you'll be seen as an intern who is wise beyond their years:

1. *When you can, file by date.* Most people make the mistake of filing paper by project names in alphabetical order. In some cases, when one is filing materials related to a subject that is truly ongoing, this makes sense. However, for most information, it's better to file things chronologically. Time is the only real standard measure we have – this is why

newspapers and magazines and blogs are always indexed by date. The other advantage of filing by date is that it's easier to get rid of the oldest stuff when it becomes obsolete.

2. *Don't file anything that is mass produced or available online.* Every time you're about to file something ask, "If I didn't have this particular piece of paper, could I find it easier elsewhere?" If the answer is yes, you don't need to keep it.

3. *Don't keep multiple copies.* This seems obvious, but sometimes people are lazy and, rather than pull out one example from a pile of copies, they will save time by just filing a pile with 50 copies of the same document.

4. *Don't file a hard copy of something you have digitally.* If you have a document on the computer, there is usually no need to file a hard copy also. Sometimes there is an exception to this rule when it comes to documents with handwritten notes or signatures. But generally, if you have something digitally, get rid of the hard copy.

Of course, these days filing is more than just paper and file cabinets; maintaining digital files is often hugely overlooked, too. Perhaps because digital files don't create piles of actual paper, people have a tendency to name files by all sorts of different systems and then store them pretty randomly. Computer search functions makes organizing digital files slightly less of an issue. However, there are a lot of good reasons to be just as organized with digital files as you are with paper files.

When your digital files are organized, finding information is faster and backing up digital information is easier. Chances are, when you arrive at your internship nobody in the history of that office will have thought too much about organizing digital files. Ask your supervisor if you can help organize their digital files, especially if you don't have a lot to do right off the bat. When you're new, there is no better way to get to know an organization and the people there than by organizing their files.

If your office has the right supplies, use hanging folders in drawers to file paper. Hanging files tend not to bend under their own weight like other file systems. If your office is like most, you'll notice many files are labeled with tabs handwritten out in chicken scratch. *Be a pro – get into the habit of printing out file tabs.* You don't even need to have the fancy perforated kind with the specific computer template – just take a couple of guesses with fonts until you find a size that works when you cut it out.

Another good alternative to hanging file folders are 3-ring binders placed on shelf. Binders are especially good for filing materials on a subject that has a finite beginning and end, but must be referenced frequently. If you're filing something in a three ring binder, the most important thing is to get a 3-ring hold punch that works and is set correctly. If you're not sure where the holes are going to punch, practice first on a scratch piece of paper.

Most interns don't take the extra step of printing out a cool looking cover for a three ring binder – or figuring out how to print a cool label for the binder spine – but you can. *Take a little time and make your work look good.* Again, print out tabs for the divider labels within the binder. Small details like these may seem unimportant and that's why most interns don't think to do them, but you can. When you do, you will stand out from the intern pack.

There are many other good techniques when it comes to filing, some of which I'll discuss further on. Filing is an art unto itself (just ask a librarian), but if you master a few basic good habits when it comes to filing – those habits will carry you well through your internship and beyond.

"He listens well who takes notes.

Dante

The Mighty Pen

Want to stand out as being the most amazing intern in the world? Here's a clue: *carry a pen and paper AT ALL TIMES.*

This is one of those things that becomes second nature to most folks in the work world after a while, but isn't something most people learn in school.

When you go to a meeting, take a pen. When you're walking down the hallway and your boss stops you to describe a task she needs you to do, take out your pen. When you're talking to somebody and they mention a resource you don't know about, write it down. When you have a great idea on your way to work – take out a pen and write it down.

If you're like most new interns, or most people for that matter, you trust your mind. Don't do it. Your mind can play tricks on you. If your boss asks you to complete project blue by Thursday, chances are your mind will remember it as: complete project green by Wednesday. Even

Handwriting

You need a pen. Paper is nice, but you can get by without it. How? Write on your hand.

Sound stupid? Maybe it is. But writing on your hand is better than not writing down things at all and it can make you seem a little extreme. As in, "I'm so dedicated as an intern I'm willing to write on myself to get the job done."

The truth is, it's not that extreme. All that ink washes off pretty easily. But when it comes time for your internship supervisors to consider whether you were truly dedicated, their memory of you writing on your hand in a pinch might actually make you look good.

if you remember correctly, your boss may not.

But, if you are a super intern who carries the mighty pen – you can win by writing things down. If there is ever a discrepancy between what somebody else says and what you remember – you can win by taking out your notes.

If nothing else, the simple act of writing down information will help you remember things correctly. *Subconsciously, when you write things down your mind starts to work on solutions.*

At the very least, writing things down during a meeting gives you something to do.

When someone is speaking and you write things down, it is a sign of respect to the person who is thinking. By writing things down, you display that not only are you present – but you care about what the speaker is saying and you find their words valuable.

Any supervisor with high standards will demand that their staff write things down. If you are the one intern who is constantly writing things down, they will notice and you will gain their confidence more quickly.

Have you ever given your order at a restaurant and your server just memorized the order without writing things down? How did you feel about that? Research actually shows that servers who write down orders and repeat them back seem more competent and tend to get bigger tips.

You may not get many tips as an intern, but the concept still holds true. When a supervisor gives you a task, get into the habit of writing it down and then briefly restating the task as you understand it from your notes. This is a mark of a master intern.

"Here's a good thing to do if you go to a party and you don't know anybody: First take out the garbage. Then go around and collect any extra garbage that people might have, like a crumpled napkin, and take that out too. Pretty soon people will want to meet the busy garbage guy."

Jack Handey

Party Like Your Career
Depends On It

Unless your office is a real sweat shop, at some point fairly soon into your internship, you will likely be involved with some sort of office party. Chances are, you might actually be tasked with going out to get stuff for said party. But either way, in the end, it's a good bet that you will be standing shoulder to shoulder with most of the office in a social situation before you know it.

First off, and this is something I wish I'd mastered sooner during my internship and career, accept every social invitation you possibly can. Sure, you have lots of work to do. Sure, you're tired. Sure, you may not know anybody. Sure, it could be awkward. But psyche yourself into going all the same.

Why? *You will stand out.*

Most interns are intimidated as hell by office parties, so you should do the opposite. When the awkward conference room birthday party convenes – show up. First of all, the person having the birthday will notice, and appreciate it. Second, the person or people who worked to throw the party together will notice too.

On the TV show "The Office" the Party Planning Committee is a hotbed of competition and political intrigue. The show doesn't have this completely wrong. Office parties are a weird thing – definitely not something you learn about in school. Office parties are kind of an artificial environment where you're expected to socialize with people who aren't necessarily your friends, but you know them well.

Take the opportunity at office parties to (1) get free food and drink, but also (2) get to know people in the office you otherwise might never have contact with. Honestly, some of the biggest career moves I've made in my life have been the result of conversations that started at parties. *As an intern, the office party is the one place where it's ok to network, to be a little forward about where your interests lie.*

You may have the opportunity to witness intern colleagues approach staffers or bosses during the work day to inquire about when it might be possible to talk about career development. This isn't necessarily a bad thing to do – but the savvier intern will take the opportunity to raise questions like this during the office party.

In truth, office relationships are often based on work. When colleagues get together for a party, they don't want to be lame and talk about work; but then, they really don't have much to talk about. The Office Party is a perfect occasion for you to get to know staff better and for them to get to know you and your goals.

" A meeting is an
event where
minutes are taken
and hours wasted. "

CAPTAIN KIRK

STEP 29

Let's Meet

During your career you will likely never get more out of meetings than you will as an intern.

Some may disagree, but in my humble opinion, most office meetings are too long and kind of a waste of time in terms of accomplishing work. If one adds up all the salaries of people attending a meeting and then multiplies that by the length of a meeting, the cost of a meeting can be pretty staggering.

That being said, as an intern – even if you're not accomplishing work by being in a meeting, you're at least learning about office life through osmosis.

Especially when you're new, you may not be invited to many meetings. But, if/when you are included in a meeting, you might not know some things that you'll wish you did.

As I explained earlier, for the love of Pete, bring something to write with, and be prepared to take notes. As I also explained earlier, be on time – even if you are the first person to arrive.

Whether people are actually conscious of it or not, when it comes to meetings, there is a pecking order to who sits where. If you're in a new place or a new situation and you're not sure where to sit – just stand until somebody gives you a hint about where you ought to sit. If you are shunted to the far end of the room, don't take offense. As an intern – especially as a new intern – people assume you will likely have the least to contribute; they will seat you accordingly.

This goes back a little bit to the FNG thing. Where you sit in a meeting is an indication of status. Status is a function of whether you've earned your spurs. Be respectful by not presuming that you are entitled to sit in the middle of things, and people will think better of you for not being presumptuous.

Once you find a place to sit or stand or whatever, unless you're expecting a call from the President or something really important, put your cell phone on buzz. If the room is boiling hot, don't sit there sweating like a dork, take off your jacket. If other people have drinks, its fine for you to have a drink too.

If you find yourself in a long, long meeting, excuse yourself if you need to. If you find yourself falling asleep – it's better to excuse yourself and leave rather than risk falling asleep during a meeting. Come up with a fake reason if you need to.

The good thing about attending meetings as an intern is that you can learn a lot. The bad thing is, until you wind up being more involved, you may need to be a fly on the wall for a little while.

When Meetings Go Wrong

If you're in an endless meeting and you don't feel like you're learning anything or adding anything valuable, and you have a ton of other work to get done – don't hesitate to get the hell out of there. Just because you are an intern doesn't mean your time isn't valuable.

How do you escape from an endless meeting? Just stand up and walk out. As far as anybody in the room knows you might have another commitment, or you might be going to the bathroom, or you might be about to barf. If you're truly not adding value to the meeting, people won't worry too much about it and chances are they will be jealous because they're not having much fun in that meeting either.

“ Why does it say
paper jam when
there is no paper
jam? I swear to
God, one of these
days, I'm going to
just kick this
piece of shit out
the window. ”

SAMIR NAGHEENANAJAR

I Can't Do It!
She's Breakin' Apart!

As an intern, one device you may have the opportunity to become very well acquainted with is: the photocopier.

It's not an environmentally friendly creature, and it's not particularly cooperative – but as a new intern – you should try and make friends with this beast.

The photocopier has some relatives – they're called "printer" and the very old, but wise, "fax machine." *The smart intern makes friends with all three.*

One way you can make photocopier, printer, and fax like you (and make others in the office like you, too) is to feed them every day. Most people forget to feed these machines – don't be like other people. Photocopier, printer, and fax want paper every morning – so fill them up. Don't over fill them with paper, because that will cause them to jam. *Give them just enough to fill their drawers.*

The best way to learn about office machines is to work with them. As a new intern – try to learn everything you can about making office machines work. The main problem most modern printers, fax machines, and copiers face revolve around paper jams. Get familiar with all the doors and latches that open these machines up to the world – you'll be surprised at where paper jams can hide.

If this all sounds weird or too complicated, don't get freaked out. Getting paper out of a machine is actually pretty easy, but most interns are intimidated by it. Realize that you're not going to break these machines, so open them up wide and see if you can fix things.

Standard operation procedure for most interns facing a paper jam is: this photo copier isn't working – so I'll go find another one. Don't be like this – be a problem solver. *Be the intern who notices a copier is jammed and fix it, even though you weren't the one who caused the problem.*

Printers and fax machines run out of toner. If you're working with a printer that is out of ink – open it up and shake the hell out of the toner cartridge. This will likely get the printer through another couple of hundred more pages (be careful though – don't get ink on yourself messing with the toner cartridge).

During your internship, find out where new toner cartridges are kept and help your office stay on top of whether they need to order more. Know how to swap out new toner cartridges for old. FYI - most new cartridges require that you pull out a paper tab before they will work.

Find out what your office does with old toner cartridges. Often times there is some kind of recycle procedure that involves more than just tossing them in the trash.

In my experience, there is something about office machines that are like intern kryptonite. Interns who run into trouble with copiers and printers give up way too soon. If an office machine is giving you trouble, tangle with it. *Be the intern who is a tenacious problem solver and people will notice.*

Does It Scan?

If you're lucky, your office will have an easily accessible scanner. But if you don't have access to a scanner, but really need to email a document that you have only on paper – consider retyping it into the computer. It's not a particularly efficient use of time, but sometimes it's the easiest thing to do if you need to convey a message about information you only have on paper.

If you type at a reasonable speed, you can knock out a couple of pages in less time than you might imagine.

" An architect's
most useful tools
are an eraser at
the drafting
board, and a
wrecking bar at
the site. **"**

FRANK LLOYD WRIGHT

Your "Back to Internship" List

Most students, especially in elementary school, know about having a "back to school list." This is a list of school supplies they will need to bring on their first day of school. In high school and college – the list focuses more on textbooks than school supplies – but the list is still there.

When you start out as an intern, there are certain office supplies you will need. I suppose if you're working in some specialized field this list might not apply. But for survival as a general office dweller, the list below describes all the things you will need.

Get this stuff however you can – from the office supply cabinet – from stuff lying around – wherever. Once you get it, make sure folks know that you have dibs on it (label it if you need to). If your office doesn't provide this stuff, make a trip to Target or get it from home.

Here is the list:

1. *An in/out box*

    This is a must for personal organization at the office and most folks miss it. Sit it on your desk and make sure the "in" part is clearly labeled from the "out" part. Real pros have an in/out box like this and you should too. Especially as an intern, you may not use the out box much (you don't have anybody working for you yet who will check it), but put it on your desk anyway.

2. *A three hole punch that works*

    This is one of the most elusive pieces of office equipment. Get a three hole punch and practice with it on scrap paper so you know the correct settings for getting the holes just right.

3. *A highlighter*

4. *Scotch tape and dispenser*

5. *Good stapler and staples*

6. *Small container of paperclips and binder clips*

7. *White Out*

8. *Scissors*

9. *Ruler*

10. *Notebook or pad of paper*

11. *Three pens that work that you like*

12. *A pencil and a way to sharpen it*

13. *A black sharpie*

14. *Post-It notes*

"Are you bored with life? Then throw yourself into some work you believe in with all your heart, live for it, die for it, and you will find happiness that you had thought could never be yours."

DALE CARNEGIE

Don't Be Bored

One of the biggest frustrations (and unexpected situations) that most new interns experience during their internship is the circumstance of being bored and/or not having enough to do.

First off, let me just say, this is going to happen sometimes. Even the busiest person in the world with the most hectic schedule can have periods of lull where they're a little idle. However, there is a difference between the occasional slow day and feeling like you're spending your whole internship sitting around.

Whether you know it or not – there is ALWAYS SOMETHING TO DO. The trick is figuring out what that is. As an intern, there are plenty of regular, valuable tasks that need doing. From the first day of your internship, make a list of these. They may not be the most glamorous tasks, but somebody has to get credit for doing them, it might as well be you. These might include: adding paper to the machines, watering the plants, making sure the voicemail has been checked, organizing the

177

supply cabinet, cleaning the office refrigerator, organizing your boss' desk, fluffing couch pillows, organizing files on the office shared drive, etc.. You see, there is always something to do. It may not be stuff you necessarily want to do, but don't fool yourself, it's there.

The thing is, if you are the intern that is constantly doing stuff that nobody seems able to identify or willing to do, more substantive work will certainly come your way soon. *More senior staff will want to reward you for doing the not-so-glamorous stuff, and will recognize your can-do attitude.*

In the end, if you've truly hit your bottom in terms of struggling to find stuff to do, do some learning. Find ten articles related to the organization where you are interning and read them. Memorize the lyrics to a song you'd like to know. Memorize the Presidents of the United States in order. Get into the habit of bringing a book to work (or, nowadays, just load one onto your phone). The point of an internship is to get access, and learn new skills. If you're sitting at your desk and there is no access to be had right then, focus on learning – even if it's not necessarily related to your internship.

The worst (or maybe the best) thing that could happen would be for a supervisor to walk by and notice you're doing something unrelated to work. This would be an opportunity for you to remind that person that you don't have enough to do just then related to work and you're ready to help with whatever needs doing, but you don't want to waste time.

Honestly, if you are extremely idle during your internship, this is a failure of your internship program. If you suspect that a good internship program is one where interns are so busy they don't have time to see straight, you're right. However, not all internship supervisors are skilled enough to manage interns this way – you may find yourself in a situation where you are a bit idle.

If this becomes a persistent problem, you may be in a situation where your intern program is not living up to their end of the bargain. In such a case, spend some of that idle time looking for another internship where your talent might be put to better use.

PART FIVE

Communication

" Ten people who speak make more noise than ten thousand who are silent. **"**

NAPOLEON

STEP 33

Speak Up

Most interns make the mistake of chattering on about things that don't advance the work, but then when they know something of true value – they don't speak up.

If you're an intern who knows something, speak up! This assumes, of course, that you KNOW something, not THINK something – we'll get into that later. Most interns, however, get intimidated. They have good ideas, but they are afraid that somebody will think they are stupid.

Here's the thing about which I'm convinced: deep down, EVERYBODY thinks their ideas might be stupid. The difference between the average intern and the great intern (or the average/great anybody) is that the great person faces the fear, and speaks their mind anyway. *When you have an idea, say it.*

All through school we are taught to address our teachers as: "Mrs. Smith," "Mr. Johnson," "Dr. Brown," etc. But remember, the office is not school. One of the biggest tells interns have is the way they address colleagues. It comes from a good place; it comes from trying to have manners and show respect.

However, here's a little secret that nobody ever teaches in school: in the office, there are very few people that need to be addressed as Mr. or Mrs. or Dr. The choice is actually up to you whether you want to put the title in. For me, I tend to use titles for elected officials, ambassadors, religious leaders, and sometimes people who are much older than me who I greatly respect. You should make your own choice. However, I would caution you about using Mr. or Ms. on too many people.

Call colleagues by their first name – it may feel weird at first, but just do it. Calling adults by their first name makes you a grown up, too. In the end, you must realize that everybody puts their shorts on one leg at a time. If somebody's first name was good enough for their momma when they had their diapers changed, it's probably good enough for you too.

Sometimes it can be hard for new interns to know when they should respond to their supervisor verbally, or whether they should respond to their boss some other way. Here's a trick: if your boss asks you a question verbally, respond verbally. If your supervisor asks you a question in writing, respond in writing; if by email, respond by email. Get it? You can assume that if your boss attributed enough importance to an issue to raise it verbally with you, it's important enough to respond verbally too.

As a new intern, it's also sometimes unclear to whom you should respond about an issue. *If you're unsure, respond to the person who asked the question.* Especially when you have hot info, it's tempting to broadcast to a wider group. Don't do it. You may not understand the full context of the question you've been asked. Respond to the person who raised the issue with you – then you'll be on safe ground.

For example, suppose Deputy Director Bob asks you to do some research that Director Sally needs. You do the research and find some excellent stuff. If you were to take it directly to Sally, you put Bob in a tough position. Maybe Bob has some more information to add, or maybe he wants to present it to Sally in a particular way. When you circumvent Bob, you put him in a position where he responsible for a result over which he has no control. If you have any interest in doing work for Bob in the future, don't put him in this position.

You may be under the impression that people in an office don't curse. This would be incorrect. Some of the most respected, powerful, admired people in the world curse like bandits. Should you curse in the office as an intern? It depends on the culture of your office and, of course, your own personality. But in general, I think you should.

When you curse it shows several things: (1) you're being genuine, (2) you have passion, and (3) you're not too afraid about what other people think. To somebody supervising you, these are all pretty good qualities to display.

Now, don't get me wrong….you may not want to use every expletive in the book when you're trying to impress a customer or constituent on behalf of your internship employer. However, don't feel like you need to whitewash your personality in order to score points during your internship. *Be passionate and be real, and people will want to work with you.*

When it comes to the spoken word in the office, there is one other important issue to consider. Among your friends, you may be in the habit of referring to others with terms of affection: "sweetie," "honey," etc. Realize that this is a no-no in the office, especially when dealing with members of the opposite gender. Even if you mean these terms in a completely harmless way, people can interpret them as being disrespectful – don't use them. "Buddy," "friend," "comrade"…words like that are totally fine – just avoid the amorous stuff.

Along those lines, be careful about commenting about colleagues' appearance – especially those of the opposite gender. You might think this is predominately an issue of men speaking about women, but trust me, it goes both ways. It's fine to tell somebody they look nice, or maybe even that you like a certain aspect of their outfit – but unless you know somebody really well – just avoid this area, especially as an intern.

If somebody looks like they've gained weight, are pregnant, wearing a wig, has a lazy eye – don't say a damn thing about it – at least not in the office!

" One if by land,
two if by sea. **"**

PAUL REVERE

Secret Language

People in an office, or pretty much any organization for that matter, tend to naturally form a tribe. As such, they tend to develop their own secret language.

Slang, acronyms, abbreviations, etc. are all ways that people in an organization and distinguish themselves from those outside an organization. Being at work is sometimes like being a member of secret club. As a new intern, you are the FNG - the new inductee of the club. *If you want to make progress, you better get hip to office lingo.*

Every office is different, and the cool lingo changes over time. But here are some phrases you can use that will make you sound cool. Even if these terms aren't used in your particular office, people will recognize them as cool office-talk that must come from someplace. If you speak more like an office pro and less like an intern, people will treat you more like an office pro.

1. *Push Back*

   Meaning: to resist an idea or action; "Alice felt very strongly that we should make the offer now, but I pushed back."

2. *Pull the trigger*

   Meaning: to launch; "Are we ready to pull the trigger on this program, or not?"

3. *Pull the plug*

   Meaning: to end; "This initiative sucks, let's pull the plug on it."

4. *Crashing*

   Meaning: very busy; "I can't talk right now, I'm crashing."

5. *Offline*

   Meaning: away from the group; "Rather than take up everybody's time on this conference call, let's take this issue offline."

6. *Needs more work*

   Meaning: not ready yet; "This idea is good, but the proposal needs more work."

7. *The paper*

   Meaning: document, any written material; "Do you have the paper about next week's event?"

8. *Radioactive*

   Meaning: something that is messed up, or somebody who messed up such that they are now untouchable; "Fred stole money from the company to support his gambling habit, and he was caught being mean to puppies; he's radioactive now."

9. *Hand holding*

Meaning: reassurance; "I've never pulled off an event this big before... I need a little hand holding."

10. *Breakup*

Meaning: no longer willing to deal with/engage; "They've called me five times, with five different answers. I'm breaking up with them."

11. *Heavy lift*

Meaning: a difficult task; "Most of the work has already been done so it shouldn't be too much of a heavy lift."

12. *Low hanging fruit*

Meaning: easy tasks that are high impact; "Before we make this heavy lift, let's go after the low hanging fruit."

13. *Not there yet*

Meaning: not ready; "I think we should have a conversation eventually, but we're just not there yet."

" I get mail; therefore I am. "

SCOTT ADAMS

You've Got Mail

One could devote an entire book to the art of office email etiquette – but for sanity's sake, let me put forth the most important things you should know about email in the workplace. These are things that most interns don't know.

Chances are, as a new intern, you're likely coming from a younger and more e-savvy generation than most of your work counterparts. As such, you are probably wired to be more casual about email than you should be, at least at work.

When somebody emails you at work with a question, you should email them back – preferably sooner rather than later. Ideally, you email back with an answer to their question. Avoid responding with an "I'll check that" answer unless you know it will take too long to get the actual answer. In other words, don't email an "I'll check that" response, and then 5 minutes later send the answer....just send the actual answer.

If somebody challenges you on email, but you believe you are right, respond. No response implies that you yield. However, don't ever email anything that you wouldn't want seen by everyone. Heated discussions about work over email are fine, just so long as you don't get personal. *Never email somebody in anger, and avoid getting in fights over email.* If you get angry over email, you lose.

Some in the workplace treat their inbox like a river where they catch some things that go by, but are resigned to miss others. Don't be like this. *Even in settings where you might get hundreds of emails/day – be on top of everything and delete anything you don't need immediately.* Shoot to get your email down to one screen. In other words, no more than 20 or 25 emails pending.

If you're becoming overwhelmed by email – take the time to unsubscribe or block stuff you don't want. When you need to cut down the number of messages in your inbox, use the sort by subject function to lop off all but the newest version of every email string. *Sometimes it can be helpful to print out an email as a reminder to take action on it, and then delete that message in your inbox.*

When you're out of the office, some people make a big deal about posting an automated out-of-office message. It's fine to turn on your out of office notice, unless of course you're going to have access to a blackberry. When I email somebody and get their out of office message, I assume they are away. Then, if I get a blackberry message from them…well, it's just kind of dorkish thing to do.

Especially among young eager beaver staffers (read: interns), there isn't a good sense about when to send emails. With blackberry technology, emails aren't nearly the passive form of communication they used to be. Nowadays, if I receive an email at 9 pm on a Saturday – I feel a little pressured to reply right then. *So, avoid sending non important, non-urgent emails after hours.* If you need to, go ahead and write the email, but then use the delayed send function to send it.

Another aspect of emailing that a lot folks new to office life neglect is their signature line. *Use that signature line to put your name, title, and contact info.* If you want to be really groovy – stick a URL in there that makes you look cool (LinkedIn page, even a Facebook page if it fits the context, etc.). *Avoid random quotes or weird calligraphic fonts in your signature line.*

The Power of the P.S.

What happened to the P.S.? Back in olden days (read: before email), adding a P.S. after a signature of a letter was more common. Perhaps because it's so easy to change text with a computer now (as opposed to how difficult it was when people wrote letters by hand), the P.S. has fallen out of favor.

However, when you send email during your internship, you can use the P.S. to your advantage. For whatever reason, people will skim through the text of an email, but they tend to read the P.S. – just because it's something they don't see that often. So, when you're send emails during your internship, put some really important stuff in the P.S.

When you do, it will make your communication more effective and will make you a more effective intern.

P.S.   Remember to use a P.S.

Bonus tip: as an intern, be mindful about the title you list in your email signature line. You don't need to hide the fact that you are an intern. But at the same time, in some contexts - especially when working with people outside your office - you don't necessarily need to advertise it, either. Consider listing your title as "Assistant"; it's not untruthful…you are acting as an assistant in your office. But, it also avoids people from the outside world dismissing you as "just an intern." Titles can sometimes be touchy things. You don't want to lie about your title; on the other hand, you don't need to go out of your way to handicap yourself in your email signature line, either.

I don't know about you, but when I get an email with a neon background and yellow letters – it makes me want to take anti-seizure medication. *Keep a white background and use a standard font like Times New Roman or Arial – if you want to be really nifty, use Verdana.* Some people in the office have bad eyes – use a reasonable font.

If you're emailing with somebody who sends you a message in large font, especially an older person – do them a favor and email them back in the same font. They're not trying to shout at you on email – they are writing in a font they can see. Respond the same way.

Another aspect of email that people in the office often get wrong is Reply All. If somebody in the office emails a whole list about who can attend Bob's birthday party…you don't need to reply all back to let everybody know that you can't make it because you're getting a wart removed. Let the original sender know that you won't be able to attend, and leave it at that.

When one replies to an email with an attachment, most email programs default to dropping the attachment. Just be aware that when you reply – take the 15 seconds to copy that original attachment back into your reply. You'll be saving any future recipients the time it would take to go back through their email to find the original attachment.

66 I have gone on
the air and
announced my
telephone number
at the
Washington Post. 99

Bob Woodward

Reach Out and Touch Someone

Can you believe there was a time before email…when people had to rely on just phones and mail? Actually – there was a time before phones and mail too – but that is too medieval to even think about – so we'll just consider phones for now.

With email now more than mainstream in the workplace, phone etiquette is definitely becoming a lost art. During the 12 years of my career, I've seen the way folks operate on the phone steadily decline. For the new intern in the office, not much is expected in terms of phone skills – if you show even the slightest ability for handling yourself on the phone, you'll stand out like a sore dialing finger.

When you answer a phone at work, come up with standard way of doing it that sounds professional. If you've ever seen the reality TV show "Flipping Out," Jeff Lewis makes all his workers answer the phone by saying, "Hello! It's a great morning/afternoon/evening at Jeff Lewis' Office!" Jeff Lewis has the right idea.

Unless you live under a box completely off the grid of civilization, you don't need me to convince you how phone skills are at an all-time low. In my experience, it's not unusual that I need to ask somebody to repeat themselves when they answer the phone in order for me to figure out what the hell they just said.

When I was an intern in the First Lady's Office, I was taught - and later taught others - to answer every call clearly with "Office of the First Lady." Individual staffers would answer by saying, "This is (say your first name)."

"This is Eric" is actually how I still answer my phone today.

Come up with a standard professional way of answering your phone from the very first call you receive. When others hear you answering your phone like a professional, they will start treating you like one.

If you get somebody on the line and you need to put them on hold, ask them if they can hold (note, *ask* them – don't *tell* them to hold), then use the hold button to put them on hold! Most new interns totally get this wrong – and it's a true tell that they are newbies. When I say put a caller on hold, it doesn't mean hold the phone to your chest or whisper to your co-worker, "what do I do?" It means press down the hold button.

Make this a habit, and if you're not sure how to use the hold button – practice with somebody between two phones in the office on your first day until you can do it in your sleep.

If a second or third call comes in while you are already on the phone, again, ask your current caller if they can hold. If they can, put them on hold. Then, answer the incoming call and ask (don't *tell* them, *ask* them) if they can hold.

When I was an intern in the First Lady's Office I once asked a second caller if they could hold, and they clearly said "yes, I can hold." I finished the first call in just a moment and then came back to the second call. The second caller said, "Hi Eric, this is Hillary – can you bring over a copy of today's press clips?" I had just put the First Lady on hold – but, it was okay, because I'd asked, and she was very cool.

In the office, some folks just let incoming calls go to voicemail. However, I would encourage you to get into the habit of trying to catch all calls when they come in live, even if that means you have to ask your callers to hold sometimes. First, it's more efficient (because you don't have to call the person back and/or run the risk of playing phone message tag with them). Second, if somebody is calling you, they probably want to talk to you right then – chances are they will be okay with holding a bit in order to get you. Third, if somebody is calling, you never know when it might be urgent; voicemail might be not be good enough.

Make a habit of being reachable and you will be a more valuable asset in the workplace during your internship and beyond.

If you find yourself on the phone in a situation where you need to take a message from somebody, there is certain information you need to take down. Sometimes offices will have little message pads that you can fill out. But whether your office uses a certain phone message form or not, make sure to write down the time and date of the call. Write down the caller's name, organization, and telephone number.

Ask the caller if they want to say why they are calling. If they answer with an issue that you can resolve – help the caller yourself (this is the mark of truly excellent intern). If they don't want to say or it's something they can't address, write that down. Once you have that information, depending on the protocol of your particular office, either put it on the recipient's chair or email it to them.

If you're in an office, invariably you'll get a call that should be transferred to somebody else. The transfer always trips up new interns. Again, if you're not sure how to transfer a call on the phones in your office, do some practice runs with phones in your office. Generally, to transfer a call on most phones you (1) hit transfer, (2) dial the new number, and (3) hit transfer again. Then, the call disappears from your phone because it has been forwarded to the other phone.

Transferring itself takes some skills that most new interns don't think about. First, when you're in your new office, find out how to dial internal calls, local calls, and long distance calls. You can be a genius at using the phone, but if you don't know how to dial the numbers, you're sunk. *Next, get a current phone list of staffers in the office and put it in a place that is readily available.* Otherwise, when the Prime Minister of Kerblakistan calls and asks to be transferred, you're going to be shuffling around looking for the right number, and the Prime Minister is going to know that you're a goof.

When a really savvy intern transfers a call, they will ask the caller something along the lines of, "If Bob isn't available, would you like their voicemail?" Depending on their answer, you can either let the call go into

Bob's voicemail, or – if Bob isn't available (he's not there or doesn't want to take the call) - you can come back to the caller and let them know.

By the way, if somebody calls for a staffer who isn't there, doesn't want to talk right then, is doing interpretive dance, whatever – the correct way to describe their situation to the caller is to say that they are "unavailable." A professional intern never says, "Beatrice isn't here" or "Beatrice is on another call right now" – it's always "Beatrice is not available right now."

I don't know what it is, but sometimes interns wind up changing the pitch of their voice on the phone. My theory is that they do this unconsciously to sound less intimidating, but whatever the case – it doesn't sound good. When you are on the phone, especially if you don't have a lot of experience on the phone

Phone Like A Land Lubber

If, during your internship, you ever need to make or receive a very important call, do everything you can to do it from a land line. Cell phone technology is amazing, but calls made through cell phones are not as clear as calls involving at least one land line.

or you're freaked out by being on the phone in a professional setting, focus on using a grown up voice. *Speak from your chest, be fearless, sound bold.*

When you call someone and get their voicemail, be very succinct with your message. The formula should be, "Hello, this is (insert your name) with (insert your organization). I'm calling about (insert subject – not the whole story – two or three words at most). If you would, please call me back at (insert your number, say it slowly). Again that number is (insert your number, say it slowly). Thank you very much." Click.

A good message shouldn't be longer than 15 or 20 seconds. When most people leave a voicemail they try and tell their life story and then end by saying their telephone number so it sounds like, "please call me back at brreeessssssssssh", and you can't understand their number because they say it so quickly. When it comes to voicemail, don't be a dork.

"Sloppy thinking gets worse over time."

JENNY HOLZER

Don't Be Sloppy

In school, you probably got tons of experience with writing papers. When most students become interns however, for some reason, all this experience kind of goes out the window.

Maybe it's an issue of context. Whatever the case may be, during your internship you should be very careful when it comes to the written word. *Don't be sloppy.*

Starting with the application you fill out, the resume you turn in, and the cover letter on top – make extra sure that you don't have any typos or spelling mistakes. Think you're good to go? Stop, look again. Challenge yourself to find the errors.

If your intern manager is a good one, they may have a habit of giving you instructions that are written down. They might hand you something with a note like this:

5/1/11: Hi, Tom. Please make the following edits and return to me. Thanks, Wilma

If you're the Tom in this situation you should make the edits carefully (again, carefully). Then print out the new version.

Before you even think about taking the paper back to Wilma, compare the marked-up version with the edited version. Look at each change edit by edit to make sure you've got them all. If/when you find a mistake – shred the version you just printed, make the change, and start again. Once you're double sure that every edit has been made, look at the new version as a whole: is the formatting still right? Does it look right in general?

Then and only then, you should paper clip Wilma's marked-up version to the new version. Next to Wilma's original instructions, you should write something like this:

5/4/11: Hi, Wilma. Edits have been made. Please let me know if you need any more changes. Thanks, Tom

If you've done a good job, Wilma should be good to go with the version you've printed. It's possible that Wilma will make some more edits and hand it back to you. If she does, that's fine. It's possible that Wilma will find an error that you missed and hand it back to you. If she does, it isn't great – but use the occasion as an excuse to make yourself be more careful next time.

When I was an intern, I had the great fortune of having a supervisor who was very patient with me. Even though I made mistakes sometimes, she didn't make a big deal about it. When you make edits for a supervisor, motivate yourself to get the edits done in one take. Can you do it? Even great interns make mistakes sometimes - the difference is how they handle those mistakes.

When a great intern makes a mistake, it pisses them off. Be like that.

Here's another tip when it comes to editing paper for your boss. Definitely include a marked up version with the edited version of anything you edit for someone else. If that marked up version comes back to you in the end – be sure to hang onto it, at least for a little while. You don't have to store it in some fancy file storage system; just put it someplace where you could get it again if you need to. You don't want to be in a position where your boss asks you to reference something they wrote down – but you've already discarded the thing they wrote on.

Again, if your boss puts written instructions on your chair, return the paper face down on their chair (unless of course they're sitting in it, in which case you should just hand it to them). If the boss hands you something, hand it back. If the boss puts something in your in box, return it to their inbox.

Avoid handing paper to people as they go by just because it is convenient to you. You never know where your supervisor is headed. They might be going to lunch, they might be going to a meeting, they might be going to the bathroom. Wherever they are going, it may not be ideal for them to carry extra paper around.

66 The body
never lies. 99

MARTHA GRAHAM

Walk Tall

Most folks spend so much time focusing on what they say that they neglect to think about how they're saying it. It has been estimated that 50% of all communication is non-verbal, and another 35% on top of that relates more to how you speak rather than what you say.

As a new intern in the office, people are looking for clues about you – spoken, or otherwise. So, be aware of your body language. Stand tall, move confidently. Over the years I've seen plenty of interns who were supremely capable, but folks dismissed them because they kind of snuck around like they were afraid to bother anybody.

Unless you're interning at a chicken farm, don't walk on egg shells.

Pay attention to how you look – do whatever you can to look like a real pro. Instead of carrying around loose paper, carry some kind of fancy -looking folder thing (doesn't have to be expensive – almost anything looks better than loose paper). As an intern, especially during

Don't Apologize For Being There

Especially if you wind up interning in a particularly intimidating place, you may feel like you're in a situation where you should be neither seen, nor heard. Sometimes twisted staffers on a power trip will do things to make interns feel like this. They won't acknowledge an intern when they walk into the room, they will make an intern stand there and wait while they are doing something else truly trivial – these are all mind games.

As an intern, you may be in situations where you have to put up with this stuff – but don't ever get yourself in a mindset where you feel you need to minimize your footprint, or apologize for being present. Indeed, that path only leads into a downward spiral giving office bullies encouragement to engage in mind games with you even more.

Instead, focus all your energy on being an awesome intern. If when you run into somebody who starts playing games to make you feel small, ignore them.

an office crisis, sometimes you need to run. But don't get rattled. Don't run just because you're rattled. *Stay focused, don't panic.*

Not too long after I moved from intern to staffer, I was charged with coordinating a short stop in Europe during one of the First Lady's foreign trips. I'd never been in charge of something like this before and I was a bit out of my depth. Deep down, I was nervous about the whole thing, and it showed.

In an attempt to stay ahead of everything, during the visit I kept rushing around. I didn't realize it at the time, but my rushing made everybody else kind of nervous, too. In the end, in my rush I managed to close a car door on one of our translator's hands. It cut her hand to the bone. Rather than help with the rest of the visit, I was summarily dispatched to help get the poor injured woman to a doctor. Her hand wound up being fine, but I felt terrible and (less importantly) I looked like a goof. *Lesson learned: don't rush, don't panic – be steady.*

If you move with confidence, people will assume that you are confident and in the end, you'll be confident. *Confident interns succeed.*

PART SIX

Special Tricks

Step #39:
The Discard Drawer

Step #40:
Start A Rolodex

Step #41:
Build A Portfolio

Step #42:
Candy Bowl

Rule #43:
Be A Mime

Step #44:
Find A Niche

Step #45:
Move Your Ass

Step #46:
Responsibility vs. Control

Step #47:
Win File

Step #48:
Don't Think

Step #49:
How To Apologize

Step #50:
Power Phrases

Step# 51:
Alpha, Bravo, Charlie

Step #52:
Top Things Most Needed
In An Office

Step #53:
Read News Clips

Step #54:
Give Cards

Step #55:
Teach Other Interns

Step #56:
Don't Give Up

" No Disassemble! "

Johnny 5

The Discard Drawer

In an office, one of your biggest challenges may be how to manage paper. Inevitably, you will often find yourself looking at a document and wondering, "Can I get rid of this, or am I going to need it later?" Your solution is: the discard drawer.

This is a drawer, preferably in your desk, where you stick documents that you might need later, but probably won't. When the drawer fills up, you pull stuff from the bottom of the stack to make more room. Depending on your paper output and the depth of the drawer, this method provides a reprieve of at least a couple of weeks for all your dubiously valuable papers.

If, the rare case occurs where you actually need something that you discarded, you just dive into the drawer and find it. Because you're tossing documents in there in reverse chronological order, the deeper you go in the pile, the farther back in time you can search.

This technique is a great way to keep your desk neat while hedging against the chance that you're getting rid of something you need.

66

It's all about
who you know.

99

STEP BROTHERS

Start A Rolodex

O nce upon a time, keeping track of people was hard. Most folks kept an address book, with names and contact info written in pencil. If a contact moved, or changed jobs – you had to erase their old info and add the new stuff. If you lost your address book, you were cooked.

No longer.

With stuff like Microsoft Outlook, Google contacts, Facebook, LinkedIn, Plaxo and all the rest, there is no excuse not to start building one hell of a contact list from the get-go. You should start this from day one of your internship.

Some people are lazy. They get a person's cell phone number or email or business card, and they don't take the 30 seconds to enter that person's info into whatever database they maintain. *This is a huge mistake.*

Some of the best contacts you make are in school, or very early in your career – make absolutely sure that you take the time to enter the contact info for people you meet.

If for no other reason, you might need a particular person's contact info handy during some unforeseen future crisis. With smart phones now being what they are – there is no excuse not to have all your contact info in one.

Where do Your Contacts Live?

Where should you keep all your contact info? This may not seem like an important question at the outset of your internship – but remember – whatever system you adopt now will likely evolve into a version of whatever system you use your entire professional life.

For keeping contacts, I've seen interns devise their own Excel spreadsheet systems; I've seen interns tape business cards into address books; I've seen them throw business cards into a shoe box. But the question of where and how to keep business contacts is one where technology is now our friend. If I were a new intern starting out now, I would definitely keep my contacts online using one of the free services that are designed to do just that. Gmail, Yahoo, Plaxo – all that stuff is pretty good. Gmail is my favorite (Gmail's tagging function is awesome), but you may have your own.

The reason I mention these online programs specifically is that they all are set up to import/export contacts through a variety of different files. Being online, these systems are accessible everywhere and you don't have to worry about backing them up. As technology changes, the ability to import/export raw data to and from new systems is key. Moreover, all these tools have places to make notes about people you meet.

If you keep your contacts in Outlook on a hard drive, or just on a portable phone – you're sunk if either those are lost. Having your contact info online lets you access it/update it pretty much wherever you go, whenever you want.

66 How's your
portfolio?

66 I'd say strong...
to quite strong. 99

MEET THE PARENTS

Build A Portfolio

Many interns are motivated to pursue and internship because they feel they don't have any professional experience.

If this applies to you, it only follows that during your internship, you should document examples of your professional experience! *This means you need to build a portfolio.*

Clearly, you don't want to be making copies of sensitive or proprietary items at work in order to cart them out of the office (ask your intern host if you're not sure whether something is okay to snag). But during your internship, keep an eye out for samples of your work that might be suitable examples for a portfolio. If you need to, mark out any sensitive data; potential future employers can often get a sense about your work product without actually needing to see names/numbers, etc.

Keep a special eye out for any examples of your work that can be conveyed through various forms of media. Make sure to get copies of any publications you helped produce, and grab examples of pictures or videos that highlight your work. During your internship, have the presence of mind to think about this stuff, and it will serve you well.

" All the candy
corn that was
ever made was
made in 1911. "

LEWIS BLACK

Candy Bowl

In an office there are many ways to be gain popularity and curry favor with others. *Keeping a candy bowl on your desk is one of the best.*

What is a candy bowl? It's just what it sounds like. Put a bowl of candy on your desk, and keep it supplied. Folks in the office who are trying to diet may avoid you, but everybody else will come like mosquitoes to a zapper. If you want to senior people in the office to learn your name and know who you are, set up a candy bowl.

Warning: when people are coming by your desk, this leads to the possibility that more people are going to wind up distracting you with idle chit-chat. This is fine, unless you're on task at that particular moment.

If you've got things to do, just let people know that they're welcome to take some candy – but you're crashing right then. They'll get the idea pretty quick.

A word about the candy: get the good stuff. It'll cost you some bucks, but if you can afford it, buy the good stuff. My friend, Josh Kirshner, actually has a technique for his candy bowl. He keeps one filled just at the bottom – so folks are more apt to take a single piece rather than clean out what's left in the bowl.

Another option: a bowl of fresh fruit. A bag of small MacIntosh apples keeps quite awhile, and will probably cost you about the same amount of money as most bulk bags of candy. This way, even the staffers watching their diet will be enticed to stop by your desk periodically!

Keep a candy bowl and you will instantly be a popular in the office. Just don't pig out too much with all that candy staring you in the face all day.

" "

MARCEL MARCEAU

Be A Mime

During your internship you can really pull off some Jedi mind tricks, if you act like a mime.

Whether they admit it or not, a ton of research shows that people tend to admire other people who are like them. Ask yourself, who are your biggest heroes in life? Chances are, a good number of them are your same gender, race, and age…they likely have a similar background to you, and have similar goals.

So, as an intern, if you're trying to get the attention of somebody in the office, be a mimic. If they hold their pen a certain way, do the same. If their posture is a certain way, do the same.

Some would call a technique like this "sucking up." Well, maybe it is, and maybe it isn't. But whatever the case, it works.

If you're a new intern who is trying to stand out above the crowd, a little technique like this can be very effective. In the end, it's pretty harmless and nobody will probably even notice what you're doing, at least consciously.

> " We will now discuss in a little more detail the Struggle for Existence. "

CHARLES DARWIN

Find A Niche

Among my advanced internship techniques, this is one of the most important. It's important both for being a successful intern, and for being successful after your internship. The technique is this: from the get go, you need to find a niche.

This is advice that I wished somebody would have emphasized more when I was first starting out. However, if you are starting out now, especially as an intern, I'm glad to share it with you.

As you think about your future goals and career path, decide what you want to do better than anybody else in the world.

This idea flies in the face of a lot of advice students receive during a standard Liberal Arts education, which encourages students to be well rounded, to be Renaissance people, to be generalists.

Things have changed. Today, the world is so interconnected that being a generalist doesn't have a lot of value. The much smarter play is to be an extreme specialist in one thing.

It doesn't really matter what you choose. You could be the world's expert in ancient Babylonian cabinet making, or Ethiopian tectonics, or Himalayan sign-language. *The important thing is you identify a niche.*

So, as your internship begins…and as you are picking up general office skills, never stop looking for a niche. Don't stop seeking an area where you could really see yourself going deep. Instead of molding yourself as the intern who is good at everything, strive to be the intern that is the best at one thing.

Deliberate Practice

Sometimes people make the mistake of confusing experiential learning with deliberate practice.

You can improve your knowledge and skills in a certain area by doing work related to that area. This is called experiential learning, and is the main reason that internships are valuable and beneficial for students. However, there is a second part to becoming a world class expert in any subject that interns and, frankly, most professionals, overlook. They forget to improve their knowledge and skills by deliberate practice.

For example, let us say you want to get better at using Adobe Photoshop. Using Photoshop for a project would be experiential learning; reading the manual would be deliberate practice. Suppose you want to become a better public speaker. Going out and giving lots of speeches would be experiential learning; working with a speaking coach would be deliberate practice.

During your internship you will likely be doing mostly experiential learning. But, as you dive into a specific niche, be sure to supplement that experiential learning with deliberate practice.

Experiential learning and deliberate practice amplify each other. The more you do one, the more you'll learn from the other and the faster you'll become the world's best in a specific area you decide to dominate.

" Speed kills. **"**

JAMES CARVILLE

Move Your Ass

During the 1992 campaign for President of the United States, Bill Clinton did something really smart. He set up a campaign operation in Little Rock, AR that quickly became known as "The War Room."

This intrepid effort was led by the "Ragin' Cajun" James Carville, who drove home the message that if the Clinton campaign just moved more quickly than their opponents, they would win.

In 1992 the cable news era was just coming of age. The folks in the War Room figured out that they could influence the news by providing the press with responses to opponents before their opponents had hardly finished delivering the charge. On top of that, with some foresight the Clinton folks would issue counter counter-responses before their opponents were able to even deliver their counter-response in the first place.

As an intern, if you have a choice between doing something quickly and doing something slowly, do it quickly.

During my internship in the White House, I was once asked to transcribe the audio recording of an interview the First Lady had just finished. Nobody said that it was urgent, but I didn't have anything else going on, so I sat down and got to work. The task was given to me around 10:30 am. I cranked for 90 minutes and handed the transcript to the Press Secretary by 12 pm.

A few minutes later, Mrs. Clinton arrived for a meeting that was about to convene in the room next to where I was working. As she arrived, the First Lady mentioned to her Press Secretary in passing that she would like to have the transcript of the interview she'd done that morning as soon as it was ready. Because I'd just finished it, the Press Secretary nonchalantly handed it to her right then.

When she asked how the work had been completed so quickly, I got the credit. Mrs. Clinton asked that I be pulled in from the room next door so she could thank me personally. She said, "Eric! You must run on caffeine. We need people like you!" A few months later I was hired on staff.

Whether your internship fuel is yoga, veganism, caffeine or whatever, unless you have a good reason to do otherwise, go fast!

"" Do what you
can, with what
you have, where
you are. ""

TEDDY ROOSEVELT

STEP 46

Responsibility vs. Control

During your internship, if somebody asks you to do something, make sure that you have the authority to get it done. In other words, don't ever let yourself be put in the position where somebody asks you to be responsible for something over which you have no control.

This is a lesson that even some of the most seasoned professionals don't really understand. Over the years in the workplace, I've often encountered people in positions of responsibility for which they have no control.

For example, suppose your intern supervisor asks you to be responsible for organizing a meeting, except that they want Bob be the one to send out all the invites. You might diligently reserve the room, put together the agendas, and print out materials for participants. As the date for the meeting approaches however, you realize that invites still haven't gone out. You ask Bob if you can help, but he says no – I'll send out the invites.

Finally, the day before the meeting, Bob sends out the invites. But it's too late, it's too short notice – nobody shows up. The meeting fails.

The meeting was your responsibility, so your boss calls you in to berate you about why it failed. You accepted responsibility for the meeting, even though you didn't have control over putting it together. *Don't let yourself be put in this position.*

Whenever somebody asks to you to take responsibility for something, but they won't give you the authority you need to accomplish the task successfully, let them know that you will be happy to take responsibility for the task, if they give you the control you need. Otherwise, you can't accept responsibility for completing the task. It's nothing personal, it's not being insubordinate; it's being honest, it's being professional.

It's called being an awesome intern. Whether your supervisor appreciates your stance at the time or not, rest assured, they likely will, later. Either way, a great deal of your sanity will be preserved.

> **"You will never win if you never begin.**

HELEN ROWLAND

Win File

You know that you are awesome. Other people know that you are awesome. You know other people know you are awesome because they tell you.

But, what about people who don't know you? How do you convince those people that you are awesome? Answer: you start a win file.

Anytime somebody says something particularly nice about your work, write it down with the date they said it. Whenever you get an email from somebody praising you and/or your work, paste the text of that email into your win file.

When you're just starting out in an internship is the time to be active when it comes to collecting testimonials. If you have a supervisor who you know thinks highly of you, don't be shy about asking them to write a letter of recommendation for you. Even offer to do a first draft for them, if that is helpful.

If you have the technology available, ask a supervisor to talk about your great work on video.

When an intern supervisor truly thinks highly of you, they are going to be grateful to you and for the work you've done. They will be more than happy to give you whatever evidence you need to document your great abilities.

Once you part ways from a supervisor, it's very difficult to get the same level of testimonial. Memories fade, people move on. *Get this stuff when/as it happens.* Build a win file. The next time you are applying for a program or job, or needing stuff to validate your skills online, or examples to list on an employee evaluation – use material from the win file. *Start collecting this information now.*

"Raise your hand if you're sure!" "

SURE DEODORANT

Don't Think

I can't tell you how many disasters have happened in human history because of the words, "I think." I do know of at least several hundred disasters that have occurred because of those words uttered by interns.

Linda asks Dave, "Dave, did that fax go through?"

Dave, "I think so."

EH-ERR! Wrong answer. Either Dave knows the fax went through, or he doesn't…there is no in-between.

When somebody asks you a question and you don't know the answer, there is only one correct answer. That answer is, "I don't know."

It's fine to follow this up with "…but I'm happy to find out." *Regardless, answering a question in the workplace with "I think" is generally a recipe for disaster.*

Some people, especially young interns trying to make a good impression, are afraid to say the words "I don't know." But, let's take a closer look at how this is kind of silly.

First off, is there anybody in the world that knows everything? No. Is there anybody in the world that knows, let's say…half of everything? No way.

In fact, I bet the average person knows far less than 1% of all knowledge. This goes back to what I was saying about finding a niche. This is why specialists can always add more value than generalists. But, I digress.

When somebody asks you a question and you don't know the answer, say, "I don't know." You might have a pretty good guess about something – and if you want to offer that information as an assumption or guess or bet, that's fine. But stipulate clearly that you don't know for sure.

On the other hand, if you do know the answer to something, don't be afraid to say it boldly. When you do, people will notice the lack of hedge in your voice, and might even ask, "Are you sure?" If you're sure, say so.

" Never ruin an
apology with
an excuse. "

Kimberly Johnson

How To Apologize

During your internship, you're going to make mistakes. They might even be huge, catastrophic mistakes. But here's the thing: everybody is human, everybody makes mistakes. So, don't sweat it too much.

When you make a mistake, make sure you say, "I'm sorry." Say it once. Mean it. Then, move on.

The mistake probably isn't as big a deal as you think it is, so there is no reason to dwell on it. If it truly is a huge deal, your best bet is to move on, do what you can to make it better, and learn from the error so it never happens again.

Some interns feel such pressure to perform well in the workplace that when they mess up, they have a tendency to apologize over and over. Don't be like this. Apologize once, and be done with it.

When you mess up, take responsibility. Don't whine. Don't come up with excuses. Own it. Let each mistake you make be a lesson on how to do better next time, acknowledge it, and move on.

Failure Is No Mistake

Sometimes people confuse mistakes with failure. As an intern, you shouldn't.

A mistake is a situation where you goof. You said you were going to do something and you forgot. You said the work was ready but page 20 was missing. You spelled the Icelandic Ambassador's name incorrectly. Those are mistakes. You should apologize when you make mistakes, once.

Failure is a situation where you attempt to achieve something, and it doesn't work.

After 10,000 failed attempts at perfecting the electric light bulb, Thomas Edison was asked how he could keep going. Edison is famous for saying, "I have not failed 10,000 times, I have found 10,000 ways *not* to make a light bulb."

Failure means you had the guts to try something risky, to try something new, that you tried to innovate. I think people, especially interns, should try to fail more often.

When you fail during your internship, don't apologize. Be proud when you fail. If somebody gives you a hard time when you fail, give them that Edison quotation.

Of course, make sure you know the difference between failing and making a mistake.

66

I'm hip,
I'm with it.

99

Dr. Evil

Power Phrases

Here are three power phrases that have been helpful to me over the years in the workplace. If you use them as an intern, you'll make people's heads spin.

1. *"I reject that."*

This is a good phrase to use when somebody is suggesting something you don't agree with, or don't want to do. Rather than get into a debate about the question at hand, you simply say, "Sorry, I reject that." The other person in the conversation won't expect this response, and they will be stunned for just a moment.

Use that moment to direct the conversation in another direction. If the subject turns back to the issue you don't want to address, just remind them that you've "rejected that," and deflect the dialogue in another direction.

2.   *"If I agreed with you, we'd both be wrong."*

This is a variation on "I reject that." It's a somewhat passive-aggressive way of disagreeing with somebody openly in a way that can throw the other party off-balance. It can create an opening for you to make a counter point, before your opponent has time to regroup.

3.   *"That sounds like a personal issue."*

This is a good phrase to use with somebody in the workplace that is going on and on about something that is not work-related, such that it's becoming a distraction.

For example, let's say Tom went camping over the weekend and he got a bunch of chigger bites. Every time you try to talk to Tom, he starts talking about the weekend, how he got all the chigger bites, how he hates chiggers, how he needs a better tent.

If you find this discourse on chiggers interesting or amusing, and it's not affecting your work, go with it. However, if all this chigger talk leaves you itching to get back on subject, you can shut Tom down by simply saying, "Tom, that sounds like a personal issue."

4.   *"Remember when…?"*

This is the phrase to use in the office with a bully.

I once had a supervisor who was pretty tough (she actually had a lot of personal issues, and liked to talk about them a lot). But she also had a tendency to pick on me just because she could.

On one occasion we were on a conference call together and there was some kind of background noise. She asked me, "Eric, are you making that noise?" I told her I was not. A short while later, she tore into me again by saying, "Eric, is that you making that noise? I think that noise must be coming from you! Is that you?" On this occasion, I'd had enough; I invoked the "Do you remember" technique.

I said, "No, I'm not making the noise. But do you remember the conversation we had just like 3 minutes ago when you asked me if I was making the noise, and I said that I wasn't making the noise? I'm thinking you must have forgotten the conversation we had, because here you are asking the very same question again. Do you remember the conversation we had, or are you just asking me the same question again for no reason?" Even when she backed down, I kept this up for a few more moments to make the point.

Obviously, this is a pretty aggressive technique. But if somebody is bullying you in the office for no reason and you want them to stop, this will work.

5.   *"My friend..."*

Sticking "my friend" or "our friends" before a subject you're about to voice criticism about is a way to show respect, even though you are leveling criticism. It softens the critic.

For example, you might say something like, "If our friend Bob hadn't knocked over the lantern, the barn might not have caught on fire." You're still pointing out that Bob started fire, but it's a way of saying you're still friends, nonetheless.

" Negative,
Ghostrider, the
pattern is full. "

Top Gun

STEP 51

Alpha, Bravo, Charlie

Here's one of the most useful things you can learn that not many people take the time to do – learn the correct NATO phonetic alphabet so when you've got a bad phone connection and you are giving out a flight confirmation code, or making sure you have an email address right, you sound cool.

Military folks know how to use "alpha, bravo, charlie, delta, echo, foxtrot, golf, hotel, india, juliet, kilo, lima, michael, november, oscar, papa, quebec, romeo, sierra, tango, uncle, victor, whiskey, x-ray, yankee, zulu." *So should you.*

" Be prepared. "

Boy Scout Motto

Top Things Most Needed
In An Office

O ver the years I've worked in a lot of different offices. In all those
offices, there are certain items that, for whatever reason, are
impossible to find.

I have no idea why these items are so elusive, but they are. *If you
keep some of this stuff handy during your internship, I can almost
guarantee that you will be the intern who saves the day at least once.*

The top things most needed in an office are….

1. *A knife*

Now please be careful with this one – don't go strolling through a
metal detector or anything with a bowie knife. However, a bigger knife
is something every office always needs (usually to cut cake). Don't get

yourself in a security situation, but if your office is one where getting a knife in isn't problematic, having a larger sized knife can save the day.

2. *Matches*

Again, going on the birthday theme…offices always seem to have a dearth of healthy pyromaniacs. There was a day when so many people smoked that acquiring fire was not a challenge. I'm glad smokers are become fewer and fewer, but that still leaves the issue of finding fire in short order just before the office birthday party. Keep a box of matches handy, and you could be a hero.

3. *Plastic spoon, forks, knife…and napkins*

People eat lunch at their desks, but they tend to run out stuff to eat with. The starving office mate desperate for a spoon to eat her yogurt at 7:30 am is a familiar sight. Keep a stash of plastic spoons, forks, and knives in your desk, and people will think you rule. Maintain a cache of napkins, salt, pepper, ketchup, and mustard , and you will truly be an intern bound for greatness. Of course the good part about all this is: you can get all this stuff for free.

4. *Band-aids*

In an office, people handle paper (at least for now they still do). Where hands touch paper, there are paper cuts. Unfortunately, nobody ever has band-aids. People at work also have a tendency to wear shoes that shred their feet, too. Again, no band-aids. Keep this rudimentary first aid supply at the ready, and you will become an intern that is literally a lifesaver.

5. *Tylenol*

…or whatever analgesic you prefer. People in offices work hard, consume tons of caffeine and sugar, and don't get enough fresh air or exercise. They get headaches. The ironic thing is that almost nobody ever has headache medicine. If you keep some handy, you'll quickly become the intern who is everybody's friend.

6. *Safety pins*

One particularly busy day during my internship in the White House, I was running around like a crazy man. Things were going pretty well until I happened to catch my pants pocket on part of door latch going through a doorway. RIIIIIIIIIIPPPPPPPP! I tore a gaping hole in my pants. There I was, standing in the White House, with my boxer shorts hanging out. Luckily, one of the staffers had a whole drawer full of safety pins. Thanks to her, I was able to patch myself together fairly well and continue the day. Ever since then, I've always made sure that I've had a good supply of safety pins – for myself, and others.

7. *Umbrella*

People in offices are busy – they don't usually pay attention to the weather as much as they should. Often, the busiest staffers are the same ones that happen to go outside a lot. These are also the same folks who never have an umbrella handy when it's raining out. I can't promise that you'll always get umbrellas returned to you, but if you're the intern who always has one handy for a colleague headed out into the rain you will likely have their gratitude.

8.   *Blank envelopes*

Offices tend to have lots of envelopes, but they are almost always ones with the organization's seal on them. When someone in the office has reason to mail something not related to the organization, they need a blank envelope. Unfortunately, these can sometimes be hard to find. Keep a stack of blank envelopes handy, and people will be amazed that you actually have some you're willing to part with.

9.   *A hammer*

It usually goes against some kind of rule, but people in offices wind up tapping little nails into the wall so they can hang pictures, or whatever they want to hang. While people can usually scrounge up little nails, they almost never have a hammer. Again, don't create a security issue, but if you're able to keep a small hammer handy in the office people will think you are some kind of "intern prophet" for your foresight.

10.   *Plastic sacks/shopping bags*

Of the items on this list, plastic bags are probably the least uncommon (people sometimes have these), but still, there are never enough of them around. If you are the intern who has a stash of shopping bags/plastic bags (especially around the holidays when people are carting around gifts and treats all the time), it will serve your cause well.

66 The reports
of my death
are greatly
exaggerated. 99

Mark Twain

Read News Clippings

Some people argue that the media is messed up, and that reading the news can only make you feel limited and depressed. I get the argument. To some degree, folks who believe this have a point.

On the other hand, if you're trying to make your way in this world as an intern, there are plenty of reasons why you should keep up with the news. First – knowing the news makes you better at conversation. When you're standing shoulder to shoulder with the big boss (the one who has the power to hire you) at the next awkward office party, being aware about the latest news in the world will give you tons to talk about.

More importantly, knowing the news will let you make little connections at work that someone less informed might miss. The time will come when you are part of conversation where a question comes up that you can answer because you stay well informed.

Especially in very busy offices, interns sometimes feel like they don't have time to read news clips or scan the web for news stories. However, the smart intern considers it part of their job to stay up to speed on the news. *You should too.*

" **When you care enough to send the very best.** "

Hallmark

Give Cards

In this age of Facebook page like, forwarded tweets, and quick emails, the old fashioned "thank you note" is becoming a rare thing, indeed. As an intern from a generation who uses old fashioned notes with decreasing frequency, you can use this to your advantage.

Before your internship even begins, get yourself a big stack of blank note cards. They don't have to be fancy – just something that looks decent that you can stick in an envelope. From the first day of your internship, look for excuses to give thank you notes. Thank staffers, thank other interns, thank clients – anybody who helps you along the way.

Now, you might be saying to yourself, "Eric! Isn't that sucking up?" Well, it IS sucking up, if that's what you do with these notes. But, that's not what I want you to do.

Send some thank you notes when you REALLY mean it. If somebody takes you to lunch, or takes the time to give you advice, or helps you

Mean It

Want to write a thank you note that will really show you appreciate the internship experience you've had, and stresses how much you would value being offered a full time position? Keep a "thank you" file right alongside the "win file" I mentioned earlier.

During your internship there will be plenty of instances where you will have reasons to feel grateful toward the people you interact with. But trust me; by the end of your internship you won't remember everything. That is, unless you make a practice of writing these instances down in a "thank you file." It can be just a simple sheet of paper, or even better, keep it as a Google Doc file.

with a project – just write out a simple thank you note. If you mean it, the note will be accepted with gratitude.

You DEFINITELY want to hand out a bunch of thank you notes if/when your internship comes to a close – or if somebody on staff leaves the office before you do. Make sure your contact information is included; you just never know when you might run into somebody again.

" **Teaching is the highest form of understanding.** **"**

Aristotle

STEP 55

Teach Other Interns

One of my favorite analogies about teaching others revolves around a staircase. When you teach something to someone else, it is like you are bringing them up to the stair on which you stand. However, when you do this, there is no room left for you on that stair. So, you must then step up onto a higher stair.

When you teach other interns, at least three things happen.

First, when you teach skills to your fellow intern, you reinforce those skills within yourself. When you teach knowledge, you become a master of that knowledge.

Second, by teaching other interns, and thereby mastering the information you teach, you prepare yourself to learn more advanced information.

Third, when you teach a fellow intern, you are building a bridge to that other intern. If you are known as the intern in the office who is willing to teach others, you will stand out not only to the other interns, but also to the staff charged with supervising them.

The willingness and ability to teach others is the true mark of a master intern.

"

Stay alive not matter what occurs! I will find you. No matter how long it takes, no matter how far, I will find you.

"

Hawkeye,
The Last of the Mohicans

Don't Give Up

Whether it's true or not, young folks today get pegged with the rap that they give up too easily. I think this comes from at least two things.

First, there has been a huge increase in focus on safety since the mid-nineties. Seat belts, car seats, bicycle helmets, rubberized playground equipment, etc...all really took off when most of today's college-age students were growing up.

Second, the Information Age took off about the same time. Among older staffers, there is a sense that with the Internet, digital music, Windows, cell phones, movies on demand, etc., today's younger set had an easier time of things.

As a new intern, older colleagues likely already have the pre-conceived notion that you are going to be prone to giving up on things too easily. *Don't let yourself play into this pre-conception.*

When you are given a task, make it a point to adopt the attitude that your ability to complete the task is not based on a question of "if," but rather, "how." Make sure that, before you concede defeat on any project, you exhaust every possible alternative route to success.

If you truly reach the point where you can't think of what to do next, go back to your intern supervisor and let them know all the things you've tried. Ask them if they have any more ideas you might try. Returning to your supervisor with this attitude is so much better than going back and saying, "I couldn't do it."

I may be biased, but I do think a lot of young people these days do give up on things too easily. Maybe it's because they never had to tape songs on the radio, or use the Dewey Decimal system; I'm not sure.

But, whatever the case, if you are the one intern in the office who gets a reputation for not giving up, you will stick out like a sore thumb. For the future prospects of a hard-working intern, standing out like a sore thumb is a very good thing.

PART SEVEN

Roadblocks

> **66** Come senators, congressmen please heed the call. Don't stand in the doorway, don't block up the hall — for he that gets hurt will be he who has stalled. **99**

BOB DYLAN

If you've read this far, I can say with complete certainty that you now know more than 99.9999% of the population about how to be a great intern. Congratulations!

It took me about 10 years to synthesize all these strategies into the formula you see here. Which means, if you implement them, you'll be about 10 years ahead of any other intern (and quite a few staffers) you encounter at work.

Here are some potential pitfalls to watch out for. Avoid these, or run the risk of not being as successful during your internship as you might:

You don't care.
There are some interns that just honest to God don't care.

You might ask, "The, why are they interning?" It could be they wanted an excuse to live away from home for the summer, or they were pressured into a program by teachers or parents. Whatever the case – since you've presumably read this far into the book – I doubt this category applies to you.

If it does, sorry – I don't really have an answer for you. If you don't care about your internship, go find something you care about.

You are afraid.

Have you ever seen one squirrel chasing another? I bet you have. If you are like me, I bet you've also noticed that there is no real reason for one squirrel to be chasing another. In fact, when the squirrel being chased decides to stand his ground to reverse the chase – a lot of times that is exactly what happens!

In other words, most squirrels are the same. The only reason one squirrel chases another is that often the chaser has just a little bit more confidence than the runner. Even when one squirrel is much bigger than the other, it really boils down to boldness and confidence. I would humbly suggest that this same phenomenon takes place among people – especially people in an office.

Don't be afraid to let these strategies work. Don't be afraid to use them.

Think you might look stupid by standing out? You might. But here is the secret: everybody is afraid they're going to look stupid. The only difference between people who step out and those who don't is the degree to which one can overcome that fear of looking stupid.

Let me make a suggestion: take all the energy that you might otherwise spend on fear, and put it into focusing on the right attitude, perfecting your office skills, fine tuning your ability to communicate, and mastering special skills.

Have extreme confidence in yourself. Here is the fun part: the more you engage in these rules, the more confidence you will have in yourself. Step into these strategies without fear, and you'll find yourself in a confidence-building feedback loop that will make you stand out. People won't see you as an intern; they'll see you as a professional.

You think you are above certain types of work.

This is a common one. You may make the decision that you are only going to do certain types of work during your internship, because some work is beneath you.

That's fine, you can think that way – but let me warn you…I don't think that is a very good strategy. Here's why:

Let's suppose you're in room, and it's you and your boss. Your boss needs two things: 1) a cup of coffee, and, 2) somebody to send an email about the Penske account. In this scenario, chances are that your boss could do the email or get the coffee, but in the allotted time…the only value you can add is: get coffee. By you going to get the coffee, resources are optimized. Results are achieved.

Now – don't get me wrong: if you're not picking up useful skills along the way and/or growing professionally…that's a different story. What I'm saying here is focus on adding value, and you will thrive in your internship. Grab any opportunity to add value in every situation, whether that means getting coffee, making copies, or hanging out with movie stars. Focus on adding value, and you can take satisfaction in knowing that the work you're doing as an intern truly matters.

You only want to do "policy."

This is a common one too. Some interns, somewhere along the way, get this meme inserted into their minds that all they want to do is "policy."

What is "policy"? Beats the hell out of me. I think people often confuse the word "policy" with "substance" to the point where they conclude that unless they are writing down thoughts on paper, the work isn't worthy.

Let me let you in on a little secret. Results achieved by pretty much any organization can be boiled down to 1) "what", and, 2) "how". In my experience, the "how" is often far more important than the "what".

Say, for example, that Charlie has a great new idea that will save an organization's clients $1,000/week. But, in order for the clients to save this money, they need to understand a five step process. If Charlie can't find a way to communicate to the clients that there is an opportunity to save money, much less convince people that it's worth their while to learn the five step process – his great idea will go nowhere. The great idea is the "what", the method for publicizing the idea and teaching people how to make it work is the "how".

So if during your internship if somebody asks you to stuff envelopes or check people into an event, or anything else that isn't strictly writing your ideas down – don't underestimate the value you can add in such situations.

You don't have any friends.

For some, doing an internship is the first time a student has done something on their own outside of school or, at the very least, apart from their peers. Some students get thrown off when they realize they are the youngest person in the office, and they really have nobody they can relate to/befriend. My advice: get over it.

I go back to the beginning of this book about the purpose of an internship, which is to gain access to special knowledge and people. Remember, if you make friends during an internship that is fine – but that is not the purpose of an internship. If you want to make friends, go to a party. Don't let lack of socializing throw you off during your internship. Get to work.

You aren't having fun.

Again, if this is your hang up – you've got the wrong focus. As Larry Winget argues in his book with the same title, "It's called work for a reason!"

If you want to have fun, go to the circus. If you want to learn and get access to people who might be able to promote your professional development, buckle down.

Bonus: if you truly challenge yourself and dig deep with an internship, chances are you will start to have fun. Being proud of the work you do is really, really fun. Trust me on this.

PART EIGHT

Be A GREAT Intern

> " **Damn the torpedoes, full speed ahead!** "

ADMIRAL FARRAGUT

If you're in school, or just beginning your career, you may not appreciate it now but you'll never have more flexibility in terms of choosing a career path than you have right now. Believe it or not, your lack of experience and degrees can be an advantage.

First, a potential employer doesn't have to worry about correcting any bad professional habits you have – because you don't have any. Second (this is good news *and* bad news for you), you are an attractive potential hire because with limited experience, they can get away with paying you less. Third, as a younger, inexperienced type they can hire you without worrying too much that you are overqualified for tasks that need to be done – but that more experienced workers might think are beneath them.

As an intern with limited experience, nobody has defined you yet. More importantly, you have yet to really define yourself professionally. However, now is the time.

If you haven't already, do some real thinking about the niche you want to make your own. Ask yourself, "What do I want to be the best in the world at?" Be extremely specific. Narrow your options. What could you like to spend the rest of your life doing? If your answer is, "I don't know," then ask yourself, "what gets me excited?"

Once you have a sense about what you'd like to be doing – go to the person or organization or place where that is done, and say, "I'm going to be your intern until I become so indispensable that you have to start paying me."

That's a little bit of an idealized/simplified strategy, but that's the basic idea of what you should do. Just because an organization doesn't advertise an internship program doesn't mean they won't consider taking you on as an intern. If the organization doing the work you'd like to do already has an internship program, that's fine too.

Either way, the point is: don't give up. Be persistent; you have nothing to lose. Remember: an internship is meant to teach you 1) specialized knowledge, and, 2) give you access. If you find an internship that can give you those two things, chances are it's worth your while.

If you're currently in an internship, I'd encourage you to think about the expectations you have for your internship. Are they realistic? Are they being met? If so, pick one of the skills I describe in Part Four and master it. Once you've mastered that skill, pick another. Consider how effectively you are communicating as an intern. Invoke some of the ideas I talk about in Part Five. Up your game with some of the special skills I discuss in Part Six. If you do, you'll be practicing intern voodoo that most people don't even consider.

Be so good that they have to hire you. Be such a great intern that they will fight tooth and nail to keep you from going away. Where you are in the course of your internship really depends on you. Be strategic about your internship – don't take it lightly. *Any internship is an opportunity; use it.*

Everyone, sometime (most likely many times) in their lives, is the newbie who must learn from others. Moving to a new town is an internship. Meeting new friends at summer camp is an internship. Going on a first date is an internship. Everyone at one time or another is an intern. *Be a great one.*

Thank you very much for reading this book. I hope the information here helps you be a great intern, and succeed massively. Let me know how these strategies work out for you. If you come up with strategies of your own, I would be very interested to hear about them. Or, feel free to ask me questions by going to my website at http://greatintern.com. I would love to hear from you!

ACKNOWLEDGEMENTS

Before this, I had never written a book. I didn't ask anybody permission to write this book. Nobody told me I was qualified to write this book. I just wrote it.

When I started writing this book, I wasn't sure where it would lead. I wasn't sure whether I would be able to pull it off. Without the support of numerous friends, colleagues, and my family - I might have failed.

To start, I would very much like to thank the legions of interns I've had over the years. So often, regardless of whether I was a good manager or not, their excellent work demonstrated to me time after time how great interns can be a force of nature when it comes to serving others and making a positive impact in the world. Thank you, my former interns. You know who you are.

I would also like to thank First Lady/Senator/Secretary Hillary Rodham Clinton for showing me what it means to be a great leader, and accepting me as one of her interns so long ago. I also want to thank all the fantastic colleagues I had the pleasure to work with over the years in

Hillary-land. It is there that I started as an intern, and learned how to be a pro. If you're reading this and you served with me in the White House, the Senate, or the State Department – I'm talking about you.

For her help and advice with this book I would especially like to thank the indomitable Lissa Muscatine for her great wisdom. I would also very much like to thank my editor and designer Cyndi Mulligan for her amazing expertise, enabling me to finally ship this work.

This book is dedicated to my parents John & Dixie Woodard – so much of what I know, who I am, and what I can do is a credit to them.

Massive appreciation goes to my sweet daughter, Piper, and my amazing son, Fletch. The only reason I was able to work on this book with two six-month-olds in house is because they are such smart, wonderful, brave, beautiful babies.

Last, I want to acknowledge that this book would not have been possible without the encouragement, inspiration, advice and love of my beautiful, smart, fearless, fantastic wife, Keri. Because of her, my life is so full, and I learn so much. I'd be her intern anytime.

ABOUT THE AUTHOR

Eric Woodard is founder of GreatIntern.com, the website that teaches students how to be great interns, and to be hugely successful during their internships.

Eric knows firsthand how tricky the path from school, to internship, to work can be. During college he transferred schools seven times (attending five different universities). After graduating from college, he wound up working for several years as a scuba instructor on Guam.

Using many of the lessons he now teaches, from this remote Pacific island Eric managed to land an internship at the White House in Washington, DC. Eric excelled during his internship, and was eventually hired onto the White House staff. He went on to create and manage a series of internship programs around the nation's capital where he's had the opportunity to mentor hundreds of student interns to massive success.

Eric has created and managed internship programs for the White House and the U.S. Senate. He's also consulted with a variety of national non-profit clients about how to create and manage successful internship programs.

Eric Woodard's philosophy about internships and experiential learning is unique because it focuses on practical steps that students can implement immediately in order to improve their chances of succeeding as interns. Eric focuses on the topics students don't learn in school, but are assumed to possess as interns. Eric Woodard offers students a way to bridge the gap.

A Note About Fonts Used in This Book

The font used for the Chapter Titles throughout this book is called Impact Label, created in 2008 by Tension Type.

The font used for the Quotations throughout this book is Bohemian Typewriter, created in 2010 by Krraaa. It is made from a Czech Remagg typewriter.

22346472R00175

Made in the USA
Charleston, SC
18 September 2013